The European Bank for Reconstruction and Development

A Comparative Analysis of the Constituent Agreement

Preface

by **Jacques Attali**

President Designate, European Bank for Reconstruction and Development

In response to the dramatic political, economic and social changes sweeping the countries of Eastern Europe in late 1989, government representatives met in January 1990 to create the first new post-cold war institution: a bank to help the countries of Central and Eastern Europe in their transition to open, market-orientated economies. By May 29, 1990, forty governments, the European Investment Bank, and the European Community, signed the Agreement Establishing the European Bank for Reconstruction and Development.

The signatories concluded the Bank Agreement with remarkable and unprecedented speed. It is true that the Bretton Woods Conference reached agreement on the Articles of Agreement of the World Bank and the International Monetary Fund in just 22 days; but preparatory work had begun years earlier. Proposals for the Inter-American Development Bank date back to before World War II, and for the International Finance Corporation and the International Development Association, to just after that war. The Agreement Establishing the Asian Development Bank took more than a year of negotiations. The World Bank opened the MIGA convention for signature only five months after formal negotiations had begun; but preparatory work and consultations with governments occurred well before those negotiations; and the idea of an international agency like MIGA dates back decades. (It was largely because of Mr Shihata's skill and leadership that MIGA was established so quickly).

Fortunately, the drafters of the Bank Agreement were able to draw on the agreements and the experience of other development banks. In his book Mr Shihata examines the provisions of the Bank Agreement, and compares them with comparable provisions in the agreements of other multilateral development banks. In many respects — in its organisation and management, and to some extent its financing — the Bank Agreement draws heavily on the Articles of Agreement of the other development banks. Mr Shihata, as General Counsel and Vice President of the World Bank, relates the World Bank's experience in interpreting similar provisions in the World Bank's Articles of Agreement. His book is bound to be a useful source of information and authority in the day-to-day activities of the Bank. It is also an important contribution to the literature on legal aspects of international financial institutions.

At the same time, the drafters of the Bank Agreement faced a novel challenge. They did not want the new bank to be *just* another development bank, which would finance conventional development projects. The Bank's goal instead would be to assist the countries of Central and Eastern Europe to recover from decades of poor economic management, and to transform economies where industry is inefficient and often energy-intensive, where outmoded methods of management and marketing restrict agricultural production, and where the infrastructure is antiquated and the environment heavily polluted. The Bank would help those countries move from a "command economy" to an economy where prices respond to market forces, and where consumer interests are protected, not by subsidies, but by reasonable regulatory measures.

The drafters of the Bank Agreements had no map for this transition. However, they knew many of the countries of Eastern and Central Europe were strongly committed to economic reform. They realized that the work force in those countries was literate and skilled, and that a significant percentage of the industrial sector was potentially competitive. Perhaps most importantly, the drafters knew the transition would have to occur with considerable speed. The political changes which have occurred and are occurring in Central and Eastern Europe would not be likely to endure if economic dislocation — certain to occur as those economies become integrated into the world economy — were serious and sustained.

The result was novel and sometimes detailed operational provisions in the Bank Agreement. In some respects the Bank is given broad powers: it can assist, for example, in regional integration. At the same time the Bank Agreement sets a special direction for the Bank. Thus, the Bank is to focus on developing entrepreneurs in countries which had stifled private initiative. It is to promote joint ventures, and take equity positions in privately owned companies, to strengthen the private sector. It can finance competitive state-owned enterprises, enabling them to restructure operations to meet international competition; but a goal of considerable importance was to encourage their privatisation. (Loans to state-owned enterprises implementing a program of privatisation were specifically exempted from a key limitation on financing of the state sector.) The Bank can and will make infrastructure loans, including loans for environmental programs, when necessary for private sector development. While the Bank can make such loans to the state sector, it is subject to specific limitations on such activities. The Bank, further, is enjoined to promote environmentally sound and sustainable development in the full range of its operations. In sum, the Bank would have a sharper focus than a typical development bank, eschewing policy based lending, and working in practical ways — by technical assistance, loans, equity investments, assistance in privatisation, joint ventures, and guarantees and underwriting where appropriate — to foster the transition to market-orientated economies.

The Bank Agreement sets the framework for the new Bank. Mr Shihata's book makes a valuable contribution to explaining that framework, particularly as it compares with the structure of the other development banks. But establishing such a framework is merely a first step. Helping the countries of Eastern and Central Europe toward a peaceable transition to market-orientated economies, where social values and democratic principles are honoured, is the major task before us.

The European Bank for Reconstruction and Development

A Comparative Analysis of the Constituent Agreement

Ibrahim F.I. Shihata
Vice President and General Counsel, World Bank
Secretary-General, ICSID

Graham & Trotman/Martinus Nijhoff
Members of the Wolters Kluwer Academic Publishers Group
LONDON/DORDRECHT/BOSTON

Graham & Trotman Ltd.
Sterling House
66 Wilton Road
London SW1V 1DE

Kluwer Academic Publishers Group
101 Philip Drive
Assinippi Park
Norwell, MA 02061 USA

First Published in 1990
Reprinted 1992

British Library Cataloguing in Publication Data
Shihata, Ibrahim F.I.
The European Bank for Reconstruction and Development: a comparative analysis of the constituent agreement.
1. International Banking
I. Title
332.15
ISBN 1-85333-482-0

Library of Congress CIP data is available

Typeset in Garamond by Cotswold Press Ltd, Oxford
Printed and bound in Great Britain by
Athenaeum Press Ltd, Newcastle-upon-Tyne

Foreword

Despite its brevity, this book is the result of an intensive effort by many staff members of the World Bank's Legal Department. It has been written in three stages within a three-month period. My role in its preparation was closer to that of a task manager, than a single author.

Upon completion of the negotiations on the text of the Agreement Establishing the European Bank for Reconstruction and Development (the EBRD Agreement), and before it was actually signed, I distributed its provisions among several World Bank lawyers, according to their respective areas of specialization, and asked each to provide a descriptive analysis of the provisions assigned to him or her and to compare them with relevant provisions in the Articles of Agreement of the International Bank for Reconstruction and Development (IBRD) and its three financial affiliates: the International Finance Corporation (IFC), the International Development Association (IDA) and the Multilateral Investment Guarantee Agency (MIGA), as well as with those of the three major regional development banks. Mr. Louis Forget covered Articles 4-6, 22-32, 37-38, and 44-57 dealing respectively with the EBRD's capital, its organization and management, suspension and termination of membership and status, privileges and immunities. Mr. Lester Dally covered Articles 20-21 dealing with borrowings and currency issues. Mr. Scott White covered Articles 16 and 36 dealing with the special reserve and the allocation of net income. Mr. Herbert Morais, covered Articles 18-19 dealing with Special Funds. Mr. Salman Salman and Ms. Natalie Lichtenstein, separately, covered the operational issues dealt with in Articles 1-2, 8-15 and 17 and Mr. Antonio Parra dealt with other miscellaneous issues related particularly to membership (Article 3) and arbitration (Article 58). This first stage of the work was completed during the month of May, 1990.

In the following month, and after the EBRD Agreement was signed on May 29, I undertook the task of reviewing the descriptive notes submitted by my colleagues, rewrote many parts of them, and added a critical analysis which included my views on the questions involved and related different provisions in the EBRD Agreement to the policy issues underlying them and to policy discussions which arose under counterpart provisions in the charters of comparable institutions. In the process, I structured the text in its present form and provided the introductory and concluding remarks. This task was concluded in early July.

The third and final stage of the work required a meticulous review of the accuracy of the statements in the text and the references in the various notes as well as ensuring that the final text is as clear, and as brief, as possible. I was greatly assisted in this latter task by Mr. Antonio Parra. Certain sub-sections were further reviewed by World Bank Legal Advisers, Mr. Christian Walser (procurement), Mr. Lowell Doud (personnel issues) and Mr. Raj Krishna (reference to GATT). Ms. Claudia Pardinas prepared the index and added to the readability of the text.

The text in its entirety was later reviewed by Mr. Hugh Scott, Associate General Counsel, Mr. Stephen Silard, Assistant General Counsel, Finance, and Mr. Sharif Hassan, Chief Counsel, EMENA Region, at the World Bank, and by Mr. Jose Camacho, General Counsel, Mr. David Khairallah, Deputy General Counsel and Mr. Maher Mahmassani, Principal Counsel, at IFC, all of whom offered useful comments.

Ms. Marie Zenni undertook the exhausting task of typing and retyping the text and, in her absence, Ms. Lan-Anh Phung typed Chapter Two.

Through this cooperative effort, the work as a whole was completed in less than three months (involving mostly work after normal working hours and during my annual leave). This may have matched the unusually fast pace by which the EBRD Agreement itself was prepared. A much longer period would have been required if I were to have prepared the text without the able assistance of my colleagues in the World Bank's Legal Department, especially Mr. Forget and Mr. Parra. The timely completion of this study is due therefore to their contribution and dedication; the views expressed and the study's shortcomings are mine alone.

While the study was written for the benefit of the World Bank's management and staff, I found it useful to give it wider circulation through this publication, especially as the issues it covers are of interest to a much wider audience. It should also provide a much needed source for a ready comparison of the texts of the agreements establishing various multilateral development institutions, with respect to the details listed in the table of contents and the index.

I am happy to present the book to the wider audience interested in its varied subjects and in particular to the legal staff of the EBRD with whom we, in the World Bank, are looking forward to productive cooperation for the benefit of the members of both institutions.

July 30, 1990 Ibrahim F.I. Shihata
Washington, D.C.

Table of Contents

List of Abbreviations

AfDB	African Development Bank
ADB	Asian Development Bank
EBRD	European Bank for Reconstruction and Development
EC	European Communities
ECU	European Currency Unit
EEC	European Economic Community
EIB	European Investment Bank
IBRD	International Bank for Reconstruction and Development
IDA	International Development Association
IDB	Inter-American Development Bank
IFC	International Finance Corporation
IMF	International Monetary Fund
MDBs	Multilateral Development Banks
MIGA	Multilateral Investment Guarantee Agency
OECD	Organisation for Economic Co-operation and Development
SDR	Special Drawing Right

Introductory Remarks

On May 29, 1990, forty countries and two European organizations (the European Economic Community (EEC) and the European Investment Bank (EIB)) signed in Paris the Agreement Establishing the European Bank for Reconstruction and Development (EBRD).[1] This event resulted from several meetings of "technical experts" and three plenary meetings held in Paris on January 15 and 16, March 8 to 11 and April 9, 1990, following the initiative by President Mitterrand of France to establish such an institution, which was strongly endorsed by the European Council on December 9, 1989.

The purpose of this paper is to analyze this Agreement and to compare its provisions with those of the Articles of Agreement of the International Bank for Reconstruction and Development (IBRD) and, where appropriate, with provisions of the charters of other international financial institutions such as the IBRD affiliates and the three comparable regional development banks: the Asian Development Bank (ADB), the Inter-American Development Bank (IDB) and the African Development Bank (AfDB). The analysis covers three main areas relevant to the activities of EBRD and similar institutions, i.e., its *financing*, its *operations* and its *organization and management*, including

1. The full text of the ERBD Agreement and its Annexes are reproduced in Appendices I – IV.

tions and its *organization and management*, including some other details pertinent to these matters. A few general remarks may be worth making before addressing these areas in some detail:

(i)The political motivation behind the creation of EBRD and its political orientation are explicitly expressed in its charter. This is clearly different from the situation in the constituent instruments of all the other above-mentioned multilateral development banks (MDBs) including the IBRD and its affiliates. The charters of these institutions specifically prohibit them and their officers from being influenced by political considerations or by the political character of their respective members.[2] By contrast, the Preamble to the EBRD Agreement emphasizes the contracting parties' commitment to "the fundamental principles of multiparty democracy, the rule of law, respect for human rights and market economics" and welcomes "the intent of Central and

2. *See* Article IV(10) and Article V(5) (c) of the IBRD Articles which, respectively, read as follows:

> "The Bank and its officers shall not interfere in the political affairs of any member; nor shall they be influenced in their decisions by the political character of the member or members concerned. Only economic considerations shall be relevant to their decisions, and these considerations shall be weighed impartially in order to achieve the purposes stated in Article I." and
>
> "The President, officers and staff of the Bank, in the discharge of their offices, owe their duty entirely to the Bank and to no other authority. Each member of the Bank shall respect the international character of this duty and shall refrain from all attempts to influence any of them in the discharge of their duties."

Similar language appears in the charters of IDA (Articles V(6) and VI(5)(c)), IFC (Articles III and IV(5)(C)), MIGA (Articles 33(c) and 34), ADB (Article 36), IDB (Article VIII(5)(d) and (f)) and AfDB (Article 38).

For further elaboration, *see* legal opinion of the IBRD General Counsel (Shihata), *Prohibition of Political Activities Under the IBRD Articles of Agreement and Its Relevance to the Work of the Executive Directors*, SecM87–1409, December 23, 1987. This, and the other legal opinions referred to in this study have limited circulation. Most of them are included in the World Bank's document *Selected Legal Opinions and Memoranda, 1983–1990* (1990).

Eastern European countries to further the practical implementation of [these principles] and their willingness to implement reform in order to evolve towards market-oriented economies". The Agreement itself includes several provisions[3] which highlight the market economy orientation of EBRD and leave no doubt as to its exclusive mandate in support of the transformation of the economic system of certain recipient countries which are committed to and actually apply specific political principles, as well as of private sector development in their territories. Instead of the typical provision explicitly excluding political considerations which appears in the Articles of Agreement of other MDBs (often under the heading "Political Activity Prohibited"), Article 32 of the EBRD Agreement only provides (under the heading "International Character of the Bank") that:

"1. The Bank shall not accept Special Funds or other loans or assistance that may in any way prejudice, deflect or otherwise alter its purpose or functions.
2. The Bank, its President, Vice-President(s), officers and staff shall in their decisions take into account only considerations relevant to the Bank's purpose, functions and operations, as set out in this Agreement. Such considerations shall be weighed impartially in order to achieve and carry out the purpose and functions of the Bank.
3. The President, Vice-President(s), officers and staff of the Bank, in the discharge of their offices, shall owe their duty entirely to the Bank and to no other authority. Each member of the Bank shall respect the international character of this duty and shall refrain from all attempts to influence any of them in the discharge of their duties."

Experience will show the extent to which non-economic considerations will play a decisive role in EBRD's practice.

3. *See* in particular, Article 1 (Purpose), Article 2 (Functions) and Article 8 (Recipient Countries and Use of Resources) elaborated on in Chapter Two, *infra*.

Its varied membership, financial and developmental nature and the expected close operational cooperation between it and the IBRD and its affiliates are factors which may enable it to function in a manner not dissimilar to that of these other institutions. Its specific and distinct mandate may, on the other hand, require it to adopt different approaches and practices especially with regard to the eligibility of recipient countries to benefit from the bank's resources. It will also be interesting to note the extent to which the new provisions in the EBRD Agreement may influence the practice of other MDBs or inspire calls for the amendment of their constituent instruments.

(ii) The EBRD Agreement is much more detailed in certain respects (especially in its Chapter III on the bank's operations) than is the case of the charters of the other above-mentioned institutions where some such details appear instead in regulations, policy papers, operational guidelines and directives issued by their competent organs and in the general conditions applicable to their loans. Incorporating such details in the constituent instrument of EBRD may have been caused by the concern that the Bank's operational policies may otherwise develop differently in practice. It may have also been based on the fact that certain policies and practices have evolved in other MDBs over the years which the drafters of the Agreement may have wanted to emphasize or deny for the new institution. It seems they were also concerned with specifying a role for the EBRD which would distinguish it from other MDBs and ensure that it would complement, rather than compete with them. While all these are valid concerns, experience shows that a detailed text, inevitably influenced by the exigencies of the time of its drafting, may cause difficulties in its implementation over time which could not be readily cured through the cumbersome amendment process.[4] A strong desire not to leave things to chance seems to have taken precedence here over considerations of appropriate drafting. When basic documents which are meant to apply for an indefinite period of time address details, rather than leaving them to the policy-making organs of the institution, undue rigidities may be built in. In addition to the detailed text of the Agreement, the Chairman of the conference which adopted it issued a report recording the understandings which the participating delegates realized were "not suitable for the Articles" but felt nevertheless that they "needed to be recorded". As summarized in the Chairman's Report, these understandings would "form part of the EBRD's basic documents, for future reference in interpreting the Articles".[5] Such understandings will no doubt have an important bearing in the application of the Agreement but cannot legally substitute for the Board of Directors' powers in interpreting its Articles.

(iii) Many of the provisions of the EBRD Agreement are identical to provisions in the charters of the IBRD or the ADB. The use of the familiar concepts and language of these instruments no doubt has advantages. However, the new text could have avoided pitfalls caused by the language of existing texts and could have benefitted more extensively from the elaborate interpretations, formal and informal, necessitated by the occasional vagueness of their language and the changing requirements of the work programs of their respective institutions. It could have avoided, as it partially did, the repetition of clauses which fell into disuse

4. In the IBRD practice over some 44 years, the Articles of Agreement, which provide for an amendment process similar to that of the EBRD, were amended only twice, once in 1966 to enable it to lend to the IFC and the second time in 1989 to increase the special majority required for further amendments.

5. *See* Chairman's Report on the Agreement Establishing the European Bank for Reconstruction and Development (referred to hereinafter as the Chairman's Report) p.1., May 29, 1990. The Chairman's Report is reproduced in Appendix V.

or proved to be unduly cumbersome in similar institutions and could have drawn on improvements introduced by more recent agreements such as the Second Amendment of the Articles of Agreement of the International Monetary Fund (IMF) and the Convention Establishing the Multilateral Investment Guarantee Agency (MIGA). The experience in the application of the Articles of Agreement of the International Finance Corporation (IFC), with its great relevance to the EBRD's activities, could also have assisted the drafters of the EBRD Agreement in formulating the provisions related to its private sector development operations, which, as it happens, are patterned to a greater extent on ADB's Articles 9 through 20.

Chapter One

Financing the EBRD: Capital Resources; Borrowings; Special Funds; Currency Issues

This Chapter deals consecutively with the EBRD capital structure (including its reserves), its borrowings, the special funds which may be entrusted to it, and various currency issues associated with its capital and with the investment of its liquid assets. It thus covers the main issues dealt with under Articles 4 to 7 and 16 to 21 of the EBRD Agreement and relates them to the provisions and experience of other MDBs, with particular reference to the IBRD's experience.

I. CAPITAL RESOURCES

1. Capital

i. Authorized Capital

The original authorized capital of the bank is "10 thousand million [i.e. ten billion] ECU", and is divided into one million shares having a par value of 10,000 ECU each (Article 4, Paragraph 1). The ECU is the European Currency Unit established by a resolution, issued on December 5, 1978, of the European Council which consists of the Heads of State or Government of the Member States of the European Communities (EC). Its value is the sum of fixed amounts of the currencies of all members of the EC. The weight of each currency in the basket, which is subject to periodic review, is determined on the basis of criteria reflecting the relative economic weight of the member currencies.[1] The ECU is at the time of writing (end of June 1990) worth about $1.24. The original capital of the bank is thus slightly larger in nominal terms than the IBRD's original capital of $10 billion, and almost fourteen times smaller than the IBRD's present authorized capital of $171 billion. The amount of the EBRD capital is subject, however, to the subsequently explained requirements of Article 6, Paragraph 3, on the method of settlement of payment obligations under the EBRD subscriptions.

The original authorized capital is divided into "paid-in shares" and "callable shares", the former having a par value of three billion ECUs, equal to 30% of the total original capital (Article 4, Paragraph 2). The EBRD's division of capital into two types of shares, paid-in and callable, follows

1. According to Article 2.1 of the 1978 resolution referred to above, the ECU is "at the centre of the EMS (European Monetary System)" created by virtue of the same resolution and elaborated on in the Basle Agreement concluded on March 13, 1979, among the central banks of the EC members. The ECU serves as the common denominator (*numéraire)* for the exchange rate mechanism known as ERIA (Exchange Rate and Intervention Arrangements) of the EC members. It is also the standard of measurement for the indicator to detect divergencies between the currencies of the EC members and is the unit of account for the intervention arrangements and certain credit transactions of the European Monetary Cooperation Fund elaborated on in the resolution. In addition, the ECU is a means of settlement between monetary authorities of the EC, and an asset held by member states of the EMS and others. At the time of writing, all members of the EC excepting Greece, Portugal and the UK are members of ERIA. Each participant in the ERIA is required to establish a central rate for its currency in terms of the ECU. Such central rates are adjustable "by mutual agreement by a common procedure" and are used to establish a grid of bilateral exchange rates. For further details, and the text of the resolutions establishing the EMS and the ECU as well as the Basle Agreement, *see* Gold, *Exchange Rates in International Law and Organization* 137–186 (1988). *See* also C. Sunt, *Legal Aspects by the ECU* (1989).

the system of the regional development banks, but contrasts with that of the IBRD. In the IBRD, it is the price of each share which is divided into a paid-in and a callable component. Both systems have proved workable in practice.

The Board of Governors will review the capital stock at intervals of not more than five years (Article 5, Paragraph 3). A similar provision appears in the IDA Articles (Article III(1)(a)) in respect of its resources, which do not take the form of share capital, and has led in practice to the replenishment of IDA resources once every three or four years since 1964. The IBRD itself now follows the practice of reviewing the adequacy of its capital resources periodically and is required, by virtue of a decision of its Executive Directors, to do so at three-year intervals.[2]

The authorized capital of the EBRD may be increased by a vote of not less than two-thirds of the Governors, exercising not less than three-fourths of the total voting power (Article 4, Paragraph 3). In the IBRD and IFC Board of Governors, the majority required to increase the authorized capital is simply three-fourths of the total voting power. In the African and Asian development banks, it is two-thirds of the Governors representing not less than three-fourths of the total voting power. In the IDB, it is a three-fourths majority of the total voting power, including two-thirds of the Governors of the regional members.

ii. Subscription of Shares

Article 5, Paragraph 1 states that each member shall subscribe shares of the EBRD capital stock "subject to fulfilment of the member's legal requirements." This language, which is not found in the charters of the other MDBs, does

2. IBRD Executive Directors' decision dated October 14, 1986 on the interpretation of the standard of value of the IBRD capital. The review by the Executive Directors is required when necessary and at any rate once every three years in order to avoid negative effects on the Bank's capital in case the SDR substantially appreciates vis-à-vis the U.S. dollar. *See* World Bank 1987 *Annual Report*, p.13.

not seem to have any effect beyond stating the obvious principle that members need to conform to their own constitutional and legislative requirements to subscribe shares in an international financial institution. Similar language used in resolutions related to capital increases in the IDB was meant in particular to allow the U.S. to make "qualified subscriptions", i.e., subject to budget appropriations by the U.S. Congress.

According to the same provision in the Agreement, each subscription to the original authorized capital stock must cover paid-in shares and callable shares in the same proportion of the totality of such shares, i.e., three to seven.

Article 5, Paragraph 1 also states that the initial number of shares "available to be subscribed" by the signatories to the Agreement shall be "that set forth in Annex A". The same paragraph adds that no member shall have an initial subscription of less than 100 shares. The initial subscriptions set forth in Annex A of the EBRD Agreement for original members may thus constitute a maximum, in the sense that original members may join the EBRD with less than the number of shares set forth in Annex A. By contrast, the statutes of the other MDBs generally provide that the number of shares set out in the Agreement constitutes the minimum initial subscription of the original members. It appears, however, that all potential members will seek authorization for subscription according to the numbers mentioned in Annex A, as was intended. Indeed, the balance provided for in the Agreement, whereby 51% of the shares (and therefore of the votes) go to the members of the European Communities (and the EEC itself and the EIB), while the U.S. acquires the largest share (10%) and Japan has a similar share to that of the four major West European countries (8.5% each), assumes that the allocated shares will be fully subscribed.

Under Article 5, Paragraph 2, the Board of Governors will determine the initial number of shares to be subscribed by non-original members. No such subscription will be authorized if it would have the effect of reducing the percentage of stock subscribed by the members of the EEC together with the EEC itself and the EIB below the 51% majority of the total subscribed capital. Similar provisions exist in the Articles of Agreement of the AfDB (Article 5(4)) and the ADB (Article 5(3)and (7)) which maintain the portion of the capital stock held by the regional members at not less than two-thirds and 60% respectively.

Article 5, Paragraph 4 authorizes the Board of Governors to increase the subscription of a member at the member's request or to allocate shares to that member within the authorized capital stock. The difference between the two actions will be clear if the first is understood to cover increases beyond the authorized capital. In either case, such an increase cannot be made if it would have the effect of reducing the percentage of stock subscribed by the members of the EEC together with the EEC itself and the EIB below the majority of the total subscribed capital.

iii. Payment and Valuation of Capital Subscriptions

The Agreement contains detailed provisions concerning the payments on shares of the initial subscriptions of the original members. While they borrow certain concepts from the statutes of other MDBs, these provisions are on the whole new.

Under Article 6, Paragraph 1, payments of the paid-in shares of the initial subscriptions of the original members are to be made in five equal instalments of 20% each. The first instalment is to be made within 60 days from the date of entry into force of the Agreement (for members which ratify it before it enters into force), and 60 days after the date of deposit of the instrument of ratification, acceptance or approval for those which become members after the entry into force (signatories of the Agreement may become members up to one year after it comes into force or within such longer period as may be decided by a slightly qualified majority of the Board of Governors specified in Article 61, Paragraph 2).

The EBRD Agreement (Article 6, Paragraph 1) further states that: "The remaining four (4) instalments shall each become due successively one year from the date on which the preceding instalment became due and shall each, subject to the legislative requirements of each member, be paid." In its Article 29, which deals with voting, the Agreement provides that in the event a member fails to pay any amount due in respect of its paid-in shares under Article 6, it "shall be unable for so long as such failure continues to exercise that percentage of its voting power which corresponds to the percentage which the amount due but unpaid bears to the total amount of paid-in shares subscribed to by that member..." The IBRD and IDA have no comparable provision, although initial subscriptions in both institutions were payable in instalments. Czechoslovakia's original membership in the IBRD was terminated after it failed to complete payment of its initial paid-in subscription. In recent IDA replenishments, authorizing resolutions provided that votes are only received as instalments of subscriptions become due and will be reduced to the extent payments are not made. In other words, votes are not given to IDA members qualifying their commitment to subscribe until payments are actually received. Initial subscriptions to IFC consisted of a single amount. In respect of *additional* subscriptions to the IFC capital, payment in instalments was authorized as an option with the proviso that the shares would be issued only upon full payment of their value.[3] No condition of this type or similar to the provision in the EBRD Agreement appears in the charters of the IDB, ADB or AfDB.

Under Article 6, Paragraph 2 of the EBRD Agreement, *half* of the amounts payable on each instalment may be paid in non-negotiable, non-interest-bearing demand notes or

3. *See* further details on this point in Chapter Three, p. 88 *infra*.

other instruments issued by the members denominated in ECU, U.S. dollars or Japanese yen, which the EBRD can draw down as it needs funds for disbursements. Demands on the notes must, "over reasonable periods of time, be made so that the value of such demands in ECU at the time of demand from each member is proportional to the number of paid-in shares subscribed to and held by each such member depositing such notes." Given the absence of a maintenance of value clause, there will be no need to introduce in the EBRD special arrangements for the denomination of such notes in ECU with a view to avoiding depreciation of their value in ECU terms.[4]

Significantly, Article 6, Paragraph 3 of the EBRD Agreement states that all payment obligations of members on the initial capital "shall be settled either in ECU, in United States dollars or in Japanese yen on the basis of the average exchange rate of the relevant currency in terms of the ECU for the period from 30 September 1989 to 31 March 1990 inclusive." That fixed value of the capital's *numéraire* is one ECU equals $1.16701, which is less than the value of the current ECU at the time of writing.

The Chairman's Report states that the initial choice between the ECU, U.S. dollar or yen made by each member would apply to payment of all instalments on the paid-in shares, "as well as to the payments made as a result of a call on the original capital". The provision on the valuation of the ECU seems to have been originally inspired by Article 5(a) of the MIGA Convention which denominates capital in

4. Following the IBRD Executive Directors' decision on the interpretation of Articles II(2) (a) and (9)(a), issued on October 14, 1986 and referred to in note 2, p. 9 *supra,* IBRD accepted payments of local currency subscriptions in notes denominated in U.S. dollars which are not subject to maintenance of value, since the U.S. dollar has become practically the standard of value of the IBRD capital. (Executive Director's decision dated June 16, 1988). More recently, the IBRD management has proposed a number of additional options to help members avoid maintenance of value settlements through repurchase of the local currency notes by U.S. dollars or their replacement by notes denominated in U.S. dollars.

terms of the SDR but defines this unit "on the basis of the average value of the SDR in terms of United States dollars for the period January 1, 1981 to June 30, 1985". Both provisions are meant to avoid the creation of an open-ended commitment for shareholders such as the U.S. which do not accept future payment obligations under their subscriptions unless they are fixed in terms of their national currency and are thus not subject to possible exchange risks. As will be further explained, the capital of IBRD is expressed in its Articles in terms of the 1944 gold dollar. This created an open-ended commitment for all shareholders in terms of their respective national currencies whenever the gold value of these currencies changed. After termination of the dollar gold value the issue has so far been solved in the IBRD through the adoption of a "fixed SDR", equal to $1.20635, as the successor of the 1944 gold dollar, by means of a formal interpretation issued by the IBRD Executive Directors.[5]

As in the case of the MIGA Convention, the EBRD Agreement does not require the members to maintain the value of their paid-in subscriptions in terms of the standard of value. Unlike the MIGA Convention, however, the EBRD Agreement authorizes payment in either of two national currencies in addition to the capital's *numéraire* which raises a further issue related to the actual burden sharing among shareholders.

If the language of the EBRD Agreement authorizing payment "on the basis of the average exchange rate of the relevant currency in terms of the ECU for the period from 30 September 1989 to 31 March 1990" were to be read along the lines of its counterpart in the MIGA Convention, it would have meant that the settlement of payments in U.S. dollars or yen as well as in the ECU itself should be made according

5. For a detailed description of the IBRD standard of value issues, *see* Shihata, "The 'Gold Dollar' as a Measure of Capital Valuation after Termination of the Par Value System: the Case of the IBRD Capital," 32 *German Yearbook of International Law* 55–86 (1989).

to the relationship between any of these *three* currencies and the fixed ECU. In other words, not only the dollar-paying and the yen-paying members would have been paying the equivalent, in either of these currencies, of the fixed ECU as defined in the Agreement, but also the members paying in ECU would have paid an amount of current ECU equivalent in value to the amount due as fixed ECU. This would have also ensured a greater equity in burden-sharing among members regardless of the currency of payment. There is no indication, however, that this meaning was intended in the final text. Rather, the term "relevant currency" which appears in Article 6, Paragraph 3 seems to be understood to refer only to the dollar and the yen, the ECU-paying members being expected to pay the nominal ECU amounts required in current ECUs without any adjustment resulting from changes in the foreign exchange value of the current ECU as compared to that of the fixed ECU.[6] The similarity in the language of the MIGA and the EBRD charters in this respect should not, therefore, lead to a confusion between their different meanings.

6. To illustrate the above difference, if the nominal amount of the total shares of a member is one million ECU, and this is read to mean one million fixed value ECUs, it would require now from the member choosing to pay in ECU but actually paying in U.S. dollars, the payment of a lesser amount in current ECUs in U.S. dollar terms, as the dollar value of the ECU is at the time of writing higher than that of the fixed ECU in the Agreement ($1.240 equivalent, rather than $1.167 equivalent). However, if the standard of value is the current ECU, without any prior determination of its foreign exchange value in terms of the U.S dollar, the full nominal amount of ECU payable by that member will have to be paid without any consideration to the fixed exchange value mentioned in the EBRD Agreement. Under the similar language in the MIGA Convention referring to a fixed SDR, the first meaning is intended and has been applied (as a member choosing to pay in SDRs would pay the dollar equivalent of the fixed SDR, not the current SDR). *See* Shihata, *MIGA and Foreign Investment*, 87–88 (1988). However, under the seemingly intended meaning for the EBRD provision, the ECU paying member is expected to pay the equivalent of the nominal current ECU amount. In such a case, there is more than one standard of value for the EBRD capital: fixed ECU for the dollar or yen paying members, and the current ECU for other members. By contrast, in MIGA the standard of value is a fixed SDR in U.S. dollar terms for all members.

To the extent a member chooses the option of payment in one of the two above-mentioned national currencies, its overall obligation on payment is fixed in that currency. In the case of the promissory notes, the full payment obligation is also fixed in the chosen currency but an actual drawdown of a proportion of the outstanding amount will represent the dollar or yen equivalent of the required ECU amount, since Article 6 Paragraph 2 specifies proportionality in drawdowns in ECU terms. This means that a dollar or yen paying member will be called upon to pay an amount in either currency equal to the ECU payment due at the time of demand,[7] but cannot ultimately be requested to pay on the promissory note as a whole any amount in excess of its total obligation in dollars or yen as expressed in the note. The same would apply to callable capital, if calls on it were ever made. In any case, the member concerned will be under no obligation to maintain the value of its obligation expressed in dollar or yen against fluctuation in the current ECU/dollar or ECU/yen exchange rate. As for the members choosing to settle payments in ECU (whether they actually pay in ECU or in its equivalent in convertible currencies) their payment obligation seems to be understood as payment of the current ECU amount (or its equivalent) representing the nominal ECU proportion of the shares due for payment, without any regard to the relationship between the current exchange value of the ECU and the fixed value mentioned in Article 6, Paragraph 3 of the EBRD Agreement.

It would seem to follow under these circumstances that the value of the capital will be affected by the use which will be made by certain members of the provisions allowing payment in dollars or yen at a fixed rate of exchange vis-à-vis the ECU. To the extent these currencies depreciate

7. While the amount due for payment in ECU will be determined at the time of demand, the equivalent amount to be paid in U.S. dollar or yen will depend on the rate of exchange between the ECU and such other currency at the time of payment. *See* also Article 6, Paragraph 8.

from the ECU value fixed by the Agreement, the actual amount of funds that the EBRD can obtain from dollar or yen paying members on the entire paid-in shares (and on callable shares) will be different from the full value of the shares expressed in ECU. Meanwhile, as the ECU paying members do not seem to be allowed to adjust their ECU payment obligations accordingly, different members will acquire membership rights (e.g. votes) at different actual or potential prices. A similar result was deemed inconsistent with the IBRD Articles of Agreement and with the concept of a uniform standard of value.[8]

The uniqueness of the relevant provisions of the EBRD Agreement may be highlighted by further elaborating on the difference between them and those of the IBRD and its affiliates. The IBRD capital is expressed in its Articles in terms of the "United States dollars of the weight and fineness in effect on July 1, 1944" (the 1944 gold dollar), which, as mentioned earlier, was interpreted after the demise of the gold valued dollar to mean "the Special Drawing Right (SDR) introduced by the Fund, as the SDR was valued in terms of United States dollars immediately before the introduction of the basket method of valuing the SDR on July 1, 1974, such value being 1.20635 United States dollar for one SDR".[9] In effect, as the value of this "1974 SDR" is fixed in U.S. dollars, the IBRD's standard of value is now fixed in terms of U.S. dollars. The IFC capital is from the beginning denominated in U.S. dollars. As mentioned earlier, the MIGA Convention expresses the value of MIGA's capital in terms of SDR, but adds that all payment obligations of members with respect to the capital stock shall be settled on the basis of a fixed value of the SDR in terms of the U.S. dollar alone ($1.082) which applies to all members. This is

8. *See* Shihata, note 5, p. 14 *supra*, at p.60, referring to a conclusion reached by former General Counsels of the IBRD.

9. Decision of the (IBRD) Executive Directors dated October 14, 1986, referred to in note 2 of this Chapter, *see* p. 9 *supra*.

tantamount in fact to stating that the standard of value of MIGA's capital is $1.082 and that payment by all members must be made on that basis. Thus, under the charters of the IBRD, as interpreted, IFC and MIGA all members excepting the U.S. may have an open-ended commitment in respect of their obligations under the subscribed shares *as expressed in their respective national currencies,* even though they all have a fixed U.S. dollar obligation. In the case of the EBRD, any member which chooses to settle in dollars or yen will have a fixed obligation in terms of the chosen currency while members choosing to settle in ECUs will have an open-ended commitment depending on the value of their respective currencies in terms of current ECU at the time of payment. The degree of such open-endedness is mitigated, however, for most of the members of the European Communities by the fact that their currencies have a central rate fixed in terms of the ECU. Members other than the U.S. and Japan and other than those whose currencies have a fixed and unchanged ECU value will still have an open-ended obligation in terms of their respective national currencies even if they choose to settle in dollars or yen. Only the U.S. and Japan (if they choose, as expected, to denominate their obligation and make their payment in their respective national currencies) and those European countries whose currencies' fixed ECU value remains unchanged will not be subject to an open-ended obligation.

As already mentioned, the EBRD Agreement's provision (Article 6, Paragraph 3), which authorizes members to settle their capital obligations in ECU, dollars or yen is meant to apply also to their obligations on the callable shares. Article 6, Paragraph 5 further provides that "calls shall be uniform in ECU value upon each callable share calculated at the time of the call." This ECU value may differ in terms of the dollar and yen value at the time of payment, thus causing a discrepancy in the total value of the obligations of members depending on the selected unit. Such a discrepancy could theoretically be avoided if all members use either the ECU, the dollar or the yen as the unit of denomination and payment. It could have been also mitigated if a member initially choosing to pay in ECU were authorized to change its obligation to either of the two other currencies depending on changes in the exchange rate between the ECU and the two other currencies. This is not the case, however. In any case, payment or denomination in ECU under the Agreement "shall include payment or denomination in any fully convertible currency which is equivalent *on the date of payment or encashment* to the value of the relevant obligation in ECU" (Article 6, Paragraph 8) (emphasis added).

iv. Preemptive Rights

Article 5, Paragraph 3 of the EBRD Agreement contains provisions giving preemptive rights to members on the occasion of increases in the authorized capital on terms generally similar to those in the Articles of the IBRD and its affiliates, except that the proportion of capital stock which is protected is related in the EBRD to the total subscribed capital (as is also the case in the ADB), while in the IBRD, the portion protected is understood to be a portion of the total *authorized* capital.[10] The difference may be significant if there is a large number of unsubscribed shares at the time the authorized capital is increased. In the latter situation preemptive rights can claim only a smaller portion of the newly authorized shares.

Preemptive rights are also provided for in the Articles of Agreement of the regional development banks. In the ADB, no preemptive rights arise with respect to an increase (or a portion of an increase) in the authorized capital if made

10. The IBRD Articles use in this respect the expression "total capital stock of the Bank", which has been interpreted in its context as a reference to the total *authorized* capital. *See* Memorandum from the General Counsel (Broches), *Proposed Increase in Capital*, R58–115, November 12, 1958, Annex B, paragraph 6, pp. 7–8.

solely to provide shares for new members or for special increases in subscriptions. In the AfDB, as well as in the IFC and MIGA,[11] preemptive rights do not arise when the authorized capital is increased solely to provide for the initial shares of a new member. A similar conclusion, if possible to reach by interpretation in the IBRD or the EBRD, would solve the apparent inconsistency between the preemptive rights provision and the need to allocate shares to new members without subjecting such shares to the preemptive rights of existing members. Such an inconsistency could be avoided if adequate unallocated shares of the authorized capital are always reserved for new members. This has not been the case however in the IBRD where the problem has been solved in practice by obtaining from existing members a waiver of the exercise of their preemptive rights when the subscription of a new member cannot be accommodated through the allocation of unallocated shares of the authorized capital.

2. Net Income: Reserves, Provisions and Surplus

The EBRD Agreement provides that the "Board of Governors shall determine at least annually what part of the Bank's net income ... shall be allocated to surplus or other purposes and what part, if any, shall be distributed" to shareholders (Article 36, Paragraph 1). Such a determination is to be made "after making provision for reserves and, if necessary, against possible losses" from its ordinary operations as indicated in Article 17, Paragraph 1 and explained below.

The text is based on its IBRD counterpart (Article V(14)) but differs from it in three respects. First, in the EBRD, allocations may occur more frequently than once a year ("at

11. *See* Article 6(1) of the AfDB Agreement and Article II(2)(d) of the IFC Articles of Agreement. *Compare* Articles 5(b) and 39(c) of the MIGA Convention.

least annually"). In the IBRD, allocations are to be made "annually", but a surplus amount may be established and allocated later on in the fiscal year (as was indeed recommended for the unallocated net income at the end of fiscal year 1990). Second, allocations in the EBRD may also be made for "other purposes" than surplus or dividends with the affirmative decision of at least two-thirds of the Governors representing at least two-thirds of the members' voting power. No allocation for such "other purposes" is permitted until the general reserve equals at least 10% of the authorized capital stock. The IBRD Articles are silent on allocation for other purposes but in practice the Board of Governors extended grants from net income to IDA annually from 1964 through 1987, to the Special Facility for Sub-Saharan Africa in 1986, and to the Debt Reduction Facility for IDA-only Countries in 1989. Finally, unlike the IBRD Articles, the EBRD Agreement explicitly mentions the possibility of establishing provisions against loan losses as an additional specific purpose reserve. The IBRD established a loan loss provision as of mid 1986. This decision, as explained below, was based on the IBRD's implied or incidental powers, not on a specific text in its Articles.

The increased flexibility of Article 36 of the EBRD Agreement therefore reflects, at least implicitly, the experience of the IBRD (and the regional development banks) in allocating net income as well as the evolution of accounting practices since the establishment of the IBRD. For example, prior to making its first transfer to IDA out of net income, the IBRD's Executive Directors felt it appropriate to issue a formal interpretation of the Articles validating such a transfer under the IBRD's implied or incidental powers.[12] The EBRD's inclusion in Article 36 of the possibility of the use

12. Decision of Executive Directors of the IBRD rendered on July 30, 1964 on Article V(14)(a). *See* also Memorandum of the Vice President and General Counsel (Shihata), *The Power of the Bank to Make Grants*, SecM85–172, February 15, 1985.

of net income for "other purposes" obviates the need for a similar interpretation.

At the same time, Article 36 which, like its counterpart in the IBRD, employs the terms "surplus" and "reserves" mentions in addition the term "general reserve" in specific applications without indicating whether "reserves" and "general reserve" are synonymous terms, as may be deduced from the context.[13]

The two accounting concepts of "reserve" and "surplus" have in the practice of IBRD been a source of occasional confusion both in the income allocation process and in reconciliation of the IBRD's financial statements with certain provisions of the Articles.[14] Early in its existence the IBRD abandoned the practice of allocating income to an account denominated as "surplus". The Board of Governors did not meet until well after the June 30 close of the fiscal year, by which time the year-end financial statements had already been prepared. Also, in 1950 an IBRD member withdrew, raising the question of whether the value of that member's shares should include a portion of unallocated net income and the possibility in such a case of precluding the Board of Governors from exercising the power to determine whether that portion should have been allocated to reserves

13. EBRD Article 36 states that no allocation of net income to other purposes and no distribution to members can be made until the general reserve equals at least 10 percent of authorized capital stock. Also, Article 17 lists the order of priority for charging losses from its ordinary operations. The fourth priority, after loan loss provisions, net income of the year and special reserve is its "general reserve and surpluses".

14. A prime example of the latter point is the determination of the IBRD's statutory lending limit under Article III(3), which requires calculation of its "unimpaired subscribed capital, reserves and surplus". On the IBRD's balance sheets, "reserves and surplus" correspond to items currently labelled General Reserve, Special Reserve, Accumulated Provisions for Loan Losses, and Accumulated Net Income—Unallocated (latter term being used for current income during the fiscal year that has not been allocated).

or distributed to members. To address this problem, commencing in 1950 net income was transferred to the reserve account now known as the General Reserve.[15] The General Reserve continues to grow through annual allocations of net income. Surplus amounts (after allocation to reserves) have been allocated since 1964 as grants to IDA and certain other recipients.

In 1986, experiencing its first protracted loan arrears and aware of the limits on the use of the Special Reserve, which will soon be explained, the IBRD established a separate accumulated provision for loan losses, as it preferred not to treat its General Reserve in part as a specific loan loss reserve.[16] The Executive Directors, through delegated power, currently decide on changes in the amount of the loan loss provision, shortly before or after the close of each fiscal year. Transfers to the General Reserve are also made by decisions of the Executive Directors, which are later on "noted with approval" by the Board of Governors. Such transfers are charged against net income. No other transfers from such income have been made to "reserve accounts"

15. That account was originally called the General Reserve Against Losses on Loans and Guarantees Made by the Bank and subsequently renamed the Supplemental Reserve Against Losses on Loans and from Currency Devaluations. In 1976, a change in U.S. accounting principles (which the IBRD follows, together with international accounting standards) cast doubt on the appropriateness of using the Supplemental Reserve as a specific reserve against loan losses, and it was redesignated the General Reserve.

16. In IBRD, but not in IDA, loan loss provisioning begins simultaneously with the move of a country to non-accrual status. No similar policy exists in ADB. In IDB, provisioning begins the month following the month in which loans are placed in non-accrual status. In AfDB a decision on whether to make provisions is made when arrears reach 24 months. In the IBRD, IDB, ADB and AfDB, loans to a borrower acquire a non-accrual status when arrears on any loan to that borrower reach a certain period (6 months for the IBRD, 180 days for the IDB, and 12 months for ADB and AfDB). Amounts of accrued, unreceived interest and charges are reversed out of income of the current period as soon as the borrower's loans are placed in non-accrual status and new income on such loans is not recognized until payments are actually received.

in the IBRD. Nor has there ever been distribution of dividends to shareholders.

Article 36 of the EBRD Agreement takes strides to improve upon the corresponding IBRD text by explicitly identifying a general reserve and a loan loss provision and by authorizing allocation of net income to purposes other than surplus. However, the simultaneous reference in the EBRD text to the dichotomy between reserves and surplus after allowing for loan loss provisioning and authorizing allocations for other purposes may raise questions regarding the role the surplus account will assume in the new institution, if such an account is going to exist at all. Allocation for other purposes also requires a special majority in the EBRD (unlike in the IBRD) which may make it a more cumbersome process. At any rate, such an allocation is not authorized in the EBRD before the general reserve reaches 10% of the *authorized* capital. The latter limitation applies also to the unlikely decision on distribution of dividends which must in any case be based on subscription payments already encashed. (Article 36, Paragraph 2, as confirmed in the Chairman's Report).

3. Special Reserve

Apart from the provisions on reserves allocated out of net income, the EBRD Agreement states that it will have a Special Reserve to be funded by commissions and fees from its ordinary operations (Article 16). This is patterned after Article IV(6) of the IBRD Articles of Agreement. However, in a significant departure from the IBRD language, the Special Reserve is kept for meeting the *losses* of the EBRD (as opposed to the *liabilities* of the IBRD). Another noteworthy distinction is that Article 16, Paragraph 2 of the EBRD Agreement expressly permits the Board of Directors to decide whether the Special Reserve is adequately funded and, if it is found to be so, to count all or part of the commissions and fees charged for its purpose as part of general income, rather than of the Special Reserve.

While the EBRD text avoids a basic problem that underlies the IBRD's Special Reserve, as noted below, a threshold question exists as to whether it was necessary for the EBRD Agreement to provide for a Special Reserve. The IBRD's Articles were drafted on the assumption that its principal activity would be to guarantee loans. To the extent the IBRD made direct loans, it was apparently envisaged that the IBRD would mostly borrow and on-lend the proceeds of its borrowings on a matched funding basis. It was contemplated that a default to the IBRD on loans or guarantees made by it would cause it to make direct payments in discharge of its matched liability, either to the creditor of the defaulting party, in the case of a guarantee, or to its direct lender in the case of a matched loan. Thus, the Articles provided that a Special Reserve would be built for the purpose of meeting IBRD liabilities caused by borrowers' default.

The IBRD evolved differently in practice and it became impractical to use the Special Reserve for the purpose stated for it, i.e. to pay to an IBRD creditor a particular obligation when an IBRD borrower delayed repayment to it. The basic business of the IBRD became direct lending, and specific loans were not tied to particular borrowings. The IBRD's financial position enabled it to have adequate resources to repay its maturing borrowings even when some delay occurred in the repayment by its borrowers of IBRD loans. In 1964, the IBRD stopped accumulating assets in the Special Reserve. The latter has become increasingly marginal to the IBRD overall reserves, with the continuous growth of the General Reserve.[17] The IBRD's Special Reserve was con-

17. Under the IBRD Articles (Articles IV(4) and (6)) the building up of the special reserve through commissions and fees was mandatory in the first ten years. At the end of FY 1990, the general reserve exceeded $9 billion while the special reserve stood at $293 million, its level since 1964.

ceived as a special component of its unique financial structure. Since in fact the IBRD acts as a direct lender routinely, that special protection, as opposed to a consolidated loan loss provision, may not have been required. The inclusion of a Special Reserve in the EBRD Agreement may also prove to be of little effect. Under EBRD Article 17, Paragraph 2, the Special Reserve would come third in priority to meet any EBRD losses, after loan loss provisions and net income. The Special Reserve would thus appear to operate as another form of loan loss provisioning, except that it will need to be maintained in a segregated account and in liquid form as the EBRD may decide. Given the relative and increasing marginality of the Special Reserve to the IBRD's operations and the inclusion in the EBRD Agreement of separate loan loss provisioning, the need for a Special Reserve for the EBRD as a subsidiary source of meeting losses may thus be called into question.

II. BORROWINGS

1. EBRD's Power to Borrow

The EBRD's power to borrow is set out in Article 20, Paragraph 1 which reads as follows:

"The Bank shall have...the power to:

(i) borrow funds in member countries or elsewhere, provided always that:
  (a) before making a sale of its obligations in the territory of a country, the Bank shall have obtained its approval; and
  (b) where the obligations of the Bank are to be denominated in the currency of a member, the Bank shall have obtained its approval...."

This provision is stated in broadly similar terms in the charters of several other MDBs. [18] The IBRD and IFC Articles require approval from the members in whose markets IBRD and IFC borrowings are made and in whose currencies the loans are denominated, but these provisions do not prevent them from borrowing in non-member countries (as, for example in Switzerland). The inclusion of the words "or elsewhere" in EBRD Article 20, Paragraph 1 explicitly permits borrowings in any country, with the approval of the country concerned. This is also the case of the ADB, IDB and AfDB charters. The broad scope of borrowing markets is particularly appropriate in institutions with a limited membership such as the regional MDBs which may need to provide access to capital markets outside that membership.

In addition to the consent of the country where the borrowing takes place (market consent), there is the further requirement for the consent of the country in whose currency the borrowing is denominated (currency consent). The IBRD, IFC and the regional MDBs have the same dual requirement. The relevance of such a requirement to an increasingly globalized financial market and in particular to borrowings denominated in freely usable currencies or international units such as the SDR and the ECU is hardly established, however. It should also be noted that the consent provision in the IBRD Articles was interpreted by the General Counsel as not necessarily being applicable to borrowings in such units as the ECU and to apply only to the country of the lead agent in case of syndicated borrowings.[19] As elaborated later on, the IBRD still seeks and obtains, in practice, approval of several countries involved

18. *See* IBRD Article IV(1)(b), ADB Article 21(i), IDB Article VII(1)(i) and AfDB Article 23(a). It should be noted that the counterpart provision of the IFC Articles (Article III(6)(i)) only requires the Corporation to seek the consent of its relevant member governments when "making a public sale of its obligations;" the requirement thus does not apply to private placements of such obligations.

19. *See* Opinion of the Vice President and General Counsel (Shihata), *Consent Requirements for ECU Borrowings by the Bank*, October 31, 1983.

in the market and in the unit of the borrowing and often gets advance approval on a blanket basis.[20]

One provision common to the borrowing provisions of the other MDBs (except IFC), but, fortunately, not included in the EBRD provisions, is the one requiring specific approval (of the member in whose markets the funds are raised, and the member in whose currency the borrowing is denominated) for exchanging the proceeds of the borrowing to the currency of any other member without restriction.[21] In the case of IDB and AfDB this further requirement is clarified as applicable to cases where funds raised are to be included in the respective bank's *ordinary* capital resources.

It should be noted in this respect that while the IBRD Articles require both a market and currency consent for funding operations, its particular provisions are unique compared with the other MDBs (including the EBRD). IBRD Article IV(1)(b) authorizes borrowing *for the purpose of lending and guarantee operations* only with the approval of the member in whose markets the funds are raised and the member in whose currency the funds are denominated and only if those members agree that the proceeds may be exchanged for the currency of any other member without restriction. In the IBRD, borrowing for other purposes is authorized by Article IV(8)(iii) which provides that, in addition to the operations specified elsewhere in the Articles, IBRD may borrow the currency of any member with the approval of that member. In other words, IBRD Article IV, Section 1(b) (borrowing for operations) requires both a market and currency consent, but its Article IV(8)(iii) (other borrowings) requires, as a matter of interpretation, only a currency consent and does not require member agreement

20. *See* p. 29 *infra*.

21. *See* IBRD Article IV(1)(b), ADB Article 21(i)(c), IDB Article IV, Section 1(i), AfDB Article 23(a)(iii).

to unrestricted convertibility of the funds raised.[22] However, in practice the IBRD did not (until the second half of 1989) make a distinction between the specific purposes of its borrowings with respect to the consent requirement and seeks both market and currency consent for each borrowing operation regardless of its purpose. Even now, as it distinguishes borrowing for lending operations from borrowing for investment purposes, the IBRD still, as a matter of policy, seeks both market and currency consent for all borrowings.

A further provision of the IBRD Articles (Article IV(8)(i)), requires consent from the member in whose territories the securities are to be bought and sold, for the purchase and sale by IBRD of its own securities, securities issued by a third party which it has guaranteed, or in which it has invested. However, the EBRD Agreement does not require a market consent for secondary market sales and purchases of securities it owns or has guaranteed, or in which it has invested (Article 20(1)(iii)).

In the IBRD, the term "currency of a member" has been understood not to include such derivative units as the ECU. Accordingly, the IBRD was deemed to be legally free to borrow in ECU without having to seek the consent of all the EEC members. It is IBRD's practice, however, to obtain consents from those members whose currencies could be selected by the IBRD fiscal agent under the borrowing as a substitute for the ECU in the event that it no longer would be used in the European Monetary System.[23]

A further issue not explicitly addressed by the EBRD's Agreement (nor by those of the other MDBs) is the position regarding consent for currency swap transactions. The IBRD was in the 1980s instrumental in developing such transactions, as well as interest rate swaps (between fixed

22. *See* Memorandum of the Legal Department, *Legal and Policy Restrictions on the Borrowing, Use and Conversion of Currencies by the Bank*, SecM88–272, March 14, 1988.

23. *See* opinion referred to in note 19, p. 28 *supra*.

and floating interest rate debts). Although they would not necessarily involve a borrowing of the currency acquired, the practice of the IBRD is to seek consent from the members whose currencies are exchanged or received in such transactions. This provides the assurance that the members involved would have no objection to the exchange of their currencies in such transactions.

2. Use of Borrowed Currencies

Under Article 21, Paragraph 2(ii) of the EBRD Agreement, members are not authorized to impose any restrictions on the receipt, holding, use or transfer of "currencies obtained by the Bank by borrowing."

This straightforward prohibition on members restricting the EBRD's use of borrowed funds may seem quite different from the more complex provisions of the IBRD Articles. It reflects, however, the understanding in practice of these latter provisions. A Memorandum of the World Bank Legal Department entitled *Legal and Policy Restrictions on the Borrowing, Use and Conversion of Currencies by the Bank*, dated March 14, 1988, describes the position in IBRD as follows:

> "Article IV, Section 2(c) provides that borrowed currencies that are received by the Bank from borrowers or guarantors on account of loan principal 'shall be held and used, without restriction by the member,' to repay the Bank's own lenders. The provision prevents all members from imposing restrictions on the Bank, such as exchange restrictions that would curtail the Bank's ability to repay its lenders or to hold and invest borrowed currencies pending their repayment by the Bank. As interpreted by the Executive Directors, the provisions of Section 2(c) do not prohibit the Bank from using any currencies received in repayment for any other purpose for which the borrowed funds could have been used, including the making of loans (Resolution No. 53, adopted on June 18, 1947).

Paragraph (d) of Article IV, Section 2 provides, inter alia, that borrowed funds 'shall be used or exchanged for other currencies or gold required in the operations of the Bank without restrictions by the members whose currencies are offered.' Whereas paragraph (c) of Article IV, Section 2 covers borrowed funds lent by the Bank and subsequently repaid to the Bank and excludes restrictions by any member on the holding and use of such currencies by the Bank, paragraph (d) covers borrowed funds pending their initial disbursement on Bank loans and excludes, but only for members whose currency the Bank holds, restrictions on the use or exchange of such currencies by the Bank. The textual differences between paragraphs (c) and (d), though difficult to explain, have not affected the Bank's operations. The Bank freely invests its borrowed funds also pending their initial disbursement; in fact, some of the Bank's borrowed funds are never disbursed on loan. As far as convertibility is concerned, Article IV, Section 1(b) and Section 2(c) and (d) all ensure that once a currency has been borrowed by the Bank with a member's approval, that member may not subsequently restrict the conversion of such currency into other currencies. Other members may not restrict the conversion of currency borrowed by the Bank that has been disbursed on Bank loans and subsequently repaid to the Bank, pursuant to Section 2(c)."[24]

Thus, the currency holdings derived from IBRD borrowings are freely usable and convertible in IBRD's operations. Only the subscriptions paid in the local currency of a member (the so-called 18% currency) are subject, for their use in lending and guarantee operations and for their convertibility, to the approval of the subscribing member. This is not the case with EBRD where, pursuant to Article 21, Paragraph 2(i), the use of holdings of ECU and the other subscription currencies is not subject to further consent by members. Thus, neither the U.S. nor Japan would be entitled to restrict the use of its national currency, paid to meet

24. Memorandum, note 22, p. 29, *supra*, at paras. 18 and 19.

its subscription obligations, if, as may be expected, it chooses to use it for this purpose, instead of the ECU.

Regarding the other MDBs, the Articles of ADB, AfDB and IDB provide in similar terms that members may not maintain or impose any restrictions on the holding or use "by the Bank or any recipient from the Bank" for payments in any country, of borrowed currencies or currencies derived from investment of those currencies.[25]

III. SPECIAL FUNDS

The EBRD Agreement includes a number of specific provisions which enable the EBRD to accept the administration of "Special Funds". There are no comparable specific provisions on special funds in the Articles of Agreement of the IBRD. The IDA Articles mention "supplementary resources" which are subject to terms and conditions to be agreed upon with the members providing them (Article III(2)). Such resources are not identified, however, as funding separate "special operations". Both the IBRD and the IDA have nevertheless in practice established special trust funds and the trend has increased in recent years, as will be shown. On the other hand, specific provisions on special funds, on which the provisions in the EBRD Agreement are closely modelled, do exist in the Articles of the ADB and the AfDB.

As will be explained in Chapter Two, the functions of the EBRD and its methods of operation are stated in greater detail than in the corresponding provisions of the IBRD Agreement, and are closer to those of the ADB and AfDB. As in the Articles of Agreement of IBRD affiliates and the regional development banks (but not the Articles of IBRD),

25. ADB Article 24(1)(iii) and (iv), AfDB Article 27(1)(c) and (d), IDB Article V(1)(b)(iii) and (iv).

Article 2 of the EBRD Agreement provides, inter alia, that the bank may "undertake such other activities and provide such other services as may further [its] functions" (Article 2, Paragraph 1(viii)).[26] Consistently with this general provision on incidental powers, Article 11 provides that one of the ways in which the EBRD shall carry out its operations in furtherance of its purpose and functions is "by deploying Special Funds resources in accordance with the agreements determining their use" (Article 11, Paragraph 1(iv)).

The term "Special Funds" is defined in Article 19 of the EBRD Agreement to include:

"(i) funds accepted by the Bank for inclusion in any Special Fund;
(ii) funds repaid in respect of loans or guarantees, and the proceeds of equity investments, financed from the resources of any Special Fund which, under the rules and regulations governing that Special Fund, are received by such Special Fund; and
(iii) income derived from investment of Special Funds resources."

The principles governing the acceptance, administration and use of such Special Funds by EBRD are provided in the EBRD Agreement in a manner broadly consistent with the IBRD practice in administering "trust funds", except for the procurement issue discussed in Chapter Two of this paper. These principles may be summarized as follows:

(a) The EBRD may only accept Special Funds "which are designed to serve the purpose and come within the functions of" the EBRD (Article 18, Paragraph 1).

26. Such incidental powers are deemed to be *implied* in the Articles of Agreement of the IBRD which do not have a similar provision but provide, in Article V(2)(f), that "the Board of Governors and the Executive Directors to the extent authorized, may adopt such rules and regulations as may be necessary or appropriate to conduct the business of the Bank".

(b) The full cost of administering every such Special Fund shall be charged to that Special Fund (Article 18, Paragraph 1).

(c) Special Funds accepted by the EBRD "may be used in any manner and on any terms and conditions consistent with the purpose and the functions of" the EBRD, and "with the other applicable provisions of this Agreement, and with the agreement or agreements relating to such Funds" (Article 18, Paragraph 2).

(d) The EBRD is required to "adopt such rules and regulations as may be required for the establishment, administration and use of each Special Fund." Here again, the EBRD is enjoined to ensure that such rules and regulations are consistent with the provisions of the EBRD Agreement (Article 18, Paragraph 3).

(e) The Special Fund resources of EBRD must "at all times and in all respects be held, used, committed, invested or otherwise disposed of entirely separately" from the resources of the bank's ordinary operations. Even the reserves of each must be kept separate in the EBRD's financial statements (Article 10, Paragraph 1). The losses and liabilities resulting from ordinary operations cannot be charged with or used to discharge losses or liabilities resulting from Special Fund operations (Article 10, Paragraph 2).

The principles set out in Article 18 of the EBRD Agreement are substantially identical to the corresponding provisions on special funds (Article 19) in the ADB Agreement, and essentially similar to the corresponding provisions (Article 8) of the AfDB Agreement.[27]

27. It should be noted, however, that under the ADB Articles of Agreement (Article 19 and 20) there are two ways of financing special funds: by external donors, as in the EBRD Special Funds, and by ADB itself, by setting aside,

The cardinal feature of the principles set out in Article 18 of the EBRD Agreement is that the EBRD may only accept, administer and use Special Funds if the terms and conditions for doing so are completely consistent with the "purpose and functions" of the EBRD and also with all applicable or relevant provisions of the EBRD Agreement.[28]

The EBRD's Special Fund resources are, according to the Chairman's Report, "assets of the Bank for the purposes of the privileges and immunities provisions of the Articles."[29] This is an important provision implied in the IBRD and IDA practices of administering trust funds, and explicitly provided for in the MIGA Convention (Article 45(c)) in respect of funds administered by MIGA.

Finally, it should be noted that the EBRD Agreement does not include any provision in respect of possible losses arising in special operations. The Chairman's Report men-

27. *cont*
according to a certain procedure, not more than 10% of its unimpaired *paid in capital* for this purpose. The resources of such funds are used in ADB to make loans or guarantees of high development priority under longer maturities, longer deferred commencement of repayment and lower interest rates than those established for ADB's ordinary operations. No similar self financed special funds are provided for in the EBRD Agreement. A question may be raised as to whether it would be appropriate for the EBRD to transfer part of its *net income* to a special fund (after the general reserve amounts to 10% of authorized capital) by the special majority required by Article 36 of the Agreement. While this may be correctly considered a transfer to one of the "other purposes" mentioned in this Article, it could raise issues related to whether it would resemble in fact a distribution of dividends to some members only, implying a waiver by other members which may need further domestic action on their part. The IBRD practice of transferring part of net income to IDA or to trust funds administered by it was considered by IBRD's auditors to be similar in nature to distribution of dividends to the benefit of all shareholders.

28. For further details, *see* Chapter Two, pp. 57-60, *infra.*

29. *See* Chairman's Report comment on Article 18, and Chapter Three, pp. 92-99 *infra.*

tions, however, in its comment on Article 17, that it was envisaged that "the Bank would make specific arrangements with the source of each relevant Special Fund in the agreement governing its use, so as to protect the separation of each type of resource in accordance with paragraph 2 of Article 10."

IV. CURRENCY ISSUES ASSOCIATED WITH INVESTMENT OF LIQUID ASSETS

Article 20 of Paragraph 1 (ii) of the EBRD Agreement provides the bank with the power to "invest or deposit funds not needed in its operations." This investment power is somewhat similar to that provided for in provisions in the charters of AfDB (Article 23(d)) and IFC (Article III(6)(ii)) except that the words "or deposit" have been added to the EBRD provision. No particular significance should be attached to this addition as bank deposits are commonly understood to be a form of investment. The provision is also similar to its counterpart in the Articles of ADB (Article 21(v)), although investment is restricted there to investment of funds in the territories of members in obligations of members or nationals thereof, and, in the case of investment of pension funds, in the territories of members in marketable securities issued by members or nationals thereof. IDB Article VII(1)(iii) qualifies its investment authority by requiring an approval by a two-thirds majority of the total voting power of members to invest surplus funds. There is no equivalent provision in the IBRD's Articles; IBRD derives its authority to invest liquid funds from its implied powers, and its charter assumes, as indicated earlier, that it may invest in securities issued by it or by a third party (Article IV(8)(i)).

As indicated earlier, Article 20, Paragraph 1(iii) of the EBRD Agreement further authorizes it to "buy and sell securities, in the secondary market, which the Bank has issued or guaranteed or in which it has invested." This provision is the same as in Article III(6)(iv) of the IFC Agreement (except for the addition of the words "in the secondary market"), and is expressed in similar terms in the charters of several other MDBs, including the IBRD.[30] However, such sales require in the case of IBRD and AfDB, the consent of the member in whose territory securities are bought and sold and in the case of ADB and IDB, the consent of the target country. By contrast, securities issued, guaranteed or bought by the EBRD, as in the IFC, can, as mentioned earlier, be sold in the secondary market without the territorial or consent restrictions applicable to the other MDBs. The Chairman's Report on the EBRD Agreement states that this provision was not intended to prevent the EBRD from using private placements or other ways of selling securities in which it had invested if an adequate secondary market in those securities did not exist.

EBRD may also "guarantee securities in which it has invested in order to facilitate their sale" (Article 20, Paragraph (iv)). This power to guarantee securities in ERBD's portfolio is expressed in identical terms in the charters of the IBRD and some other MDBs.[31] The Chairman's Report states that this authority should not be used for securities acquired for the EBRD's liquidity portfolio.

In addition, the EBRD may "underwrite, or participate in the underwriting of, securities issued by any enterprise for purposes consistent with the purpose and functions of the Bank" (Article 20, Paragraph 1(v)). The power to underwrite securities issued by the EBRD's private borrowers is the same as ADB's under its Article 21(iv). The charters of the other MDBs do not mention this underwriting power

30. *See* IBRD Article IV(8)(i), ADB Article 21(ii), AfDB Article (23)(b), and IDB Article VII(1)(ii). *See* also p. 29 *supra*.

31. *See* IBRD Article IV(8)(ii), IFC Article III(6)(iii), and IDB Article VII(1)(iv).

explicitly. The background to this provision is explained in the Chairman's Report which envisages a sparing use of this authority, but mentions that the EBRD may take up unsold shares or securities of public and private enterprises supported by the EBRD if equity or securities issued by such entities were not sold in the primary issuance. The EBRD could receive commissions for such underwritings and any shares or securities taken on to EBRD's books by this means would form part of EBRD's overall exposure in the country concerned and would be subject to any limits applicable. The Chairman's Report also points out that underwriting equity and securities issues of public and private enterprises is subject to Article 11 which authorizes such activities where other means of financing are not appropriate. Underwriting operations are also subject to the operating principles contained in Article 13 which governs the terms and conditions for loans and guarantees made by the EBRD.

Article 20, Paragraph 2 contains the requirement that EBRD place a warning on the face of its securities to the effect that they are not obligations of any government or member. This is a standard requirement for the securities issued by all other MDBs.[32] In addition, the EBRD Agreement provides in Article 5, Paragraph 7 in no unclear terms that "[n]o member shall be liable, by reason of its membership, for obligations of the Bank." This important principle is generally recognized as applicable to the other MDBs even in the absence of an explicit provision to this effect.

Finally, Article 21 enables the EBRD to make a determina-

32. *See* IBRD Article IV(9), IFC Article III(8) (which also requires the IFC warning to state that it is not an obligation of the IBRD), AfDB Article 25, ADB Article 22, and IDB Article VII(2). The importance of such a warning has been recently highlighted by the predicament of the International Tin Council (ITC). *See* Maclaine Watson & Co. Ltd. v. Department of Trade and Industry and related appeals, [1988] 3 All E.R. 257 (C.A.); [1989] 3 All E.R. 523 (H.L.). For a detailed account of the demise of the ITC, *see* Mallory, Conduct Unbecoming: The Collapse of the International Tin Agreement, 5 *Am. Univ. J. Int'l L. & P* 835-92 (1990).

tion as to whether a currency is "fully convertible", after consultation if necessary with the IMF. Similar provisions appear in the charters of MIGA (Article 3(e)), ADB (Article 23) and AfDB (Article 26(ii)) but not in the Articles of the other MDBs.

As with the IBRD, IDA and ADB Articles, the EBRD Agreement does not contain a provision on the determination of value of currencies. Typical of the provisions on this subject in the charters of the other MDBs, is Article 9 of the MIGA Convention which provides for currency valuations to be determined by MIGA after consultation with the IMF.[33]

33. Similar provisions appear in IFC Article III, Section 7, IDB Article V, Section 2, and AfDB Article 26(i).

Chapter Two

EBRD Operations: Purposes and Functions, Modes and Conditions of Operation, Suspension and Termination

Fundamental differences exist between the EBRD and the IBRD in the operations sections of their respective Articles of Agreement. Those differences stem mainly from the distinctive purposes and functions of each of the two institutions, and are conspicuously reflected in their methods of operation. While the EBRD Agreement bears in this respect some similarities to the ADB charter, and to a lesser extent, to those of the IDB and AfDB, it differs in many respects from the charters of all these other institutions and provides important innovations. This Chapter explains the main operational issues dealt with under Articles 1, 2 and 8 to 17 of the EBRD Agreement in the context of its distinct mandate, against the background of the provisions of the charters of other MDBs and the current practice of the IBRD in particular.

I. PURPOSE AND FUNCTIONS

To have a good grasp of the purpose and functions of the EBRD, one must read the Preamble of the EBRD Agreement, as well as Articles 1 (Purpose), 2 (Functions) and 8 (Recipient Countries and Use of Resources) as if they were one integral provision. The classification of the different headings below, as in the Agreement itself, should thus be seen as serving only the purposes of simplification and clarification. It should not be viewed as detracting from the integral nature of these texts and the importance of reading them together.

1. Purpose

The twofold purpose of the EBRD as briefly specified in Article 1 is "to foster the transition towards open market-oriented economies", and "to promote private and entrepreneurial initiative", both to be carried out in the Central and Eastern European countries committed to, and applying the principles of multiparty democracy, pluralism and market economies. These principles are cited in the Agreement's Preamble along with "the rule of law" and "respect for human rights". "Strengthening democratic institutions" is also mentioned in the Preamble after "the practical implementation of multiparty democracy". The message conveyed by the provisions of the Preamble and Article 1 together is clear and straightforward. While "economic progress and reconstruction" may be an ultimate objective to which the EBRD will contribute, it is not the purpose *per se*. Rather, the purpose for which EBRD was established is to assist in the great transformation of Central and Eastern European countries from a command economy controlled by a one-party political system to a new system based on a free market economy and multiparty democracy and to support the private sector development required for this transition. The new system, where respect for the rule of law and for human rights is presumed to be a fundamental requirement, assumes a reduced role of the state and an enhanced one for "private and entrepreneurial initiatives" which have therefore to be promoted.

The IBRD's purposes are stated in a more detailed but quite different manner in Article I of its charter. Those purposes include assisting in the reconstruction and development of territories of members, including the restoration of economies destroyed or disrupted by war and promoting private *foreign* investment by means of guarantees or participation in loans. The IBRD is called upon to provide financing when foreign private capital is not available on reasonable terms and, in the process, to promote the long-range balanced growth of international trade and to improve the standards of living and the conditions of labor in its member countries. In pursuing these purposes, the IBRD is required to "arrange loans made or guaranteed by it in relation to international loans through other channels so that the more useful and urgent projects ...will be dealt with first."

The IFC Articles mention the Corporation's purpose in broad terms (to further economic development by encouraging the growth of productive private enterprise in member countries, particularly in the less developed areas) and follows on this by mentioning three broad measures to be taken up in carrying out this purpose (Article 1). IDA's Articles speak also of the Association's purpose in general language (to promote economic development, increase productivity and thus raise standards of living in the less-developed areas of the world included within the Association's membership) adding only that such purpose will be served "in particular by providing finance to meet their important development requirements on terms which are more flexible and bear less heavily on the balance of payments than those of conventional loans". Both the IFC and the IDA Articles mention that their activities supplement those of the IBRD, without elaborating on the particular functions to be carried out for this purpose.

The ADB's purposes specified in Article 1 of its charter are to foster economic growth and cooperation in the region of Asia and the Far East and to contribute to the acceleration of the process of economic development of the developing member countries in the region. By comparison, the IDB's purposes are described in its charter as being simply "to contribute to the acceleration of the process of economic and social development of the regional developing member countries, individually and collectively"; the AfDB's purposes are stated in similar terms.

The comparison between the stated purposes of the several institutions clarifies that the EBRD has a distinct role, more focussed in its scope but also more ambitious than that assigned to the others. Although a financial institution, it is established to foster the strategic objective of transforming the overall system in certain countries from a command economy to a market-oriented one which also enjoys multiparty democracy. This is stated again in Article 2 and in Article 8, Paragraph 2, both of which emphasize the role of the private sector, and in particular small and medium sized enterprises. The first draft presented to the conference which negotiated the EBRD Agreement, was much broader in scope and would have enabled it to provide financing to help recipient countries with economic reforms through project finance and balance of payments support. This broad scope was restricted during negotiations where the focus was placed on the process of economic transition and on the particular measures needed to assist in this transition. The detailed provisions of Articles 1, 2, 8, 11 and 13 reflect clearly this basic orientation.

The Chairman's Report on the EBRD Agreement recognized in its comment on Article 2, Paragraph 1, that the private sector "in the potential recipient countries was at present either small or non existent" and clarified therefore that the bank "would also support the public sector in its transition from purely centralized control to demonopolization, decentralization or privatization and to a competitive business environment". Such objectives, it is to be noticed, are now being pursued by the IBRD, IDA and IFC as well, but simply as measures of economic reform based on considerations of economy and efficiency. The IFC is of course created to further economic development by encouraging the growth of productive private enterprise in its member countries (Article I of IFC's charter) but privatization of public enterprises and the broader transformation of economic systems are not specifically mentioned among its objectives or statutory functions.

The IBRD was created to assist in a different transition, the one from a wartime to a peacetime economy, and in the reconstruction and development of territories of its members worldwide. The regional banks are established to foster regional economic development without reference to either type of transition.

As indicated in Article 8, Paragraph 3, the Board of Directors of the EBRD will make sure that its resources are used for achieving the purpose mentioned in Article 1. If a recipient member implements policies inconsistent with this purpose (as well as in other "exceptional circumstances") the Board "shall consider whether access by a member to Bank resources should be suspended or otherwise modified and may make recommendations accordingly to the Board of Governors". However, the Article requires that decisions by the Board of Governors on these matters must, in view of their grave consequences, be taken by a special majority (two thirds of the Governors representing not less than three fourths of the total voting power of the members). The same majority will be needed, according to the Chairman's Report, to restore the member's access to the bank's resources. This unique provision has no parallel in the charters of other MDBs but resembles existing remedies under the Articles of Agreement of the IMF which apply under different circumstances.[1] The deprivation of access to EBRD resources should not however be confused with the suspension of all the rights of membership (except the right to withdraw) which is provided for in Article 37, as explained in Chapter Three.[2]

2. Functions

i. General

The functions of the EBRD, as stated in Article 2 of its Agreement, can be summarized as being to assist the recipient members in the achievement, on a long term basis, of the purpose of the bank described above. This specifically requires assistance in implementing structural and sectoral reforms, including demonopolization, decentralization and privatization, to help the integration of the economies of these countries into the international economy. Reference to such assistance (in structural and sectoral reform) is absent from the charters of other MDBs, although the function itself has been performed in the practice of the IBRD and IDA since the early 1980s through the extension of fast disbursing loans to countries which adopt agreed reforms.[3] The provision of the EBRD Agreement (Article 2, Paragraph 1) suggests by contrast that

1. Under Article XXVI(2)(a) of the IMF Articles of Agreement, a member that fails to meet any of its obligations under the Articles may be declared ineligible to use the Fund's general resources and such ineligibility was declared in respect of several members in arrears to the Fund. The IMF is now in the process of introducing amendments to its Articles whereby suspension of voting and related rights will be added as further remedy when, after the expiry of a reasonable period following a declaration of ineligibility, the member persists in its failure to meet any of its obligations under the Articles.

2. *See* p.81 *infra.*

3. *See* Memorandum of the IBRD Vice President and General Counsel (Shihata), *Authorized Purposes of Loans made or Guaranteed by the Bank,* SecM85-172, February 15, 1985.

assisting recipient countries in introducing structural and sectoral reform is the function of the institution, not a form of lending, and that the activities enumerated in Articles 2 and 11 of the Agreement, including lending for specific projects, are means to implement this broad function of the EBRD.[4] Such implementing measures include actions to promote the establishment, improvement and expansion of productive, competitive and private sector activity, in particular small and medium size enterprises; to mobilize domestic and foreign capital as well as experienced management to that end; to foster productive investment in a broad sense which includes the service and financial sectors necessary to support private and entrepreneurial initiatives; to provide technical assistance for the preparation, financing and implementation of relevant projects; to stimulate and encourage the development of capital markets; to support sound projects involving more than one recipient member (financing of projects involving one member are not specifically mentioned in Article 2 but should be deduced from the measures specified earlier and are covered explicitly in Articles 11 and 13 which detail methods and principles of operations); to promote, in the range of its activities, environmentally sound and sustainable development; and, as a general power, to undertake such other activities as may further the functions of the institution.

The ADB, IDB and AfDB charters, like the EBRD's, enumerate several functions and measures designed to assist in fulfilling the institution's purpose which is stated separately. Due to the different nature of these institutions, however, the specific provisions differ from one another and more so from that of the EBRD. One common provision is that which deals with technical assistance for the preparation, financing and implementation of relevant projects, a

4. *See* also pp. 60-62 *infra.*

measure commonly taken by the IBRD and IDA, but not specifically provided for in the IBRD Articles and mentioned only as a "miscellaneous operation" in the IDA charter (Article V(5)(iv)).

The separation of purposes and functions was not made in the IBRD Articles, which do not include a specific provision on "Functions" or on measures for implementing them. The IBRD's Article I on "Purposes" is drafted in such a broad manner as to include both purposes and functions. To illustrate, the EBRD's statutory *functions* include "to promote, through private and other interested investors [both domestic and foreign, according to the Chairman's Report], the establishment, improvement and expansion of productive, competitive and private sector activity" (Article 2, Paragraph 1 (i)). The IBRD's statutory *purposes* include "to promote private foreign investment by means of guarantees or participation in loans and other investments made by private investors" (Article I(1)(ii)).

The uniquely expressed purpose and functions of the EBRD will certainly guide its operations and are expected to play a major role in the application and interpretation of the Agreement as a whole. Indeed, the EBRD is required in its operations to further its stated purpose and functions (Article 11, Paragraph 1).[5] In the case of the IBRD, which is also required to be guided by its purposes in all its decisions (Article I), the objectives specified in its Articles of Agreement have been key to the legal construction of the authorized purposes of its loans and guarantees, and have provided a benchmark for permitting or prohibiting different types of operations.[6]

5. Similar provisions appear in the Articles of IDB (Article III(1)), ADB (Article 8) and AfDB (Article 2 (3)).

6. *See* Memorandum referred to in note 3, p. 45 *supra*. The same conclusion is in fact applicable to all international organizations which would be acting *ultra vires* if they deviated from their respective purposes.

In the EBRD Agreement, consistency with the purpose of the institution also provides a test of eligibility to benefit from EBRD resources. As indicated earlier, the Board of Governors, acting by special majority on the recommendation of the Board of Directors, may simply suspend a recipient country's access to such resources if the latter Board decides that such member is implementing policies inconsistent with the EBRD's purpose (Article 8, Paragraph 3). Similarly, the EBRD Agreement directs in Article 32, Paragraph 1, that the bank shall not accept Special Funds or other loans or assistance that may in any way prejudice, deflect or otherwise alter its purpose or functions.

ii. Concern for the Environment

The special emphasis on the environment which the EBRD Agreement explicitly provides deserves to be singled out in this analysis, especially as it reflects a growing concern which is not mentioned in the charters of other MDBs but is increasingly influencing their activities. As already mentioned, the measures to be pursued by EBRD include the promotion of "environmentally sound and sustainable development." This modern language, expressed in the Brundtland Commission Report[7] on the environment and development and since adopted in the published reports of the IBRD and other MDBs, seems to be particularly fitting for the EBRD recipient members where environmental problems appear to have reached unusual dimensions. The Chairman's Report recognizes the serious environmental problems in these countries and indicates that the drafters of the Agreement "emphasized that principles of environmentally sound development must be integrated into the full range of the Bank's operations", meaning this "to include all of the Bank's activities, including technical assistance and all special operations, and not merely that the Bank should

7. World Commission on Environment and Development [Brundtland Commission], *Our Common Future* (1987).

be able to provide support directly for specific environmental projects".[8] As this policy is already being followed in the operations of the IBRD and IDA, the detailed directives and procedures recently adopted by these institutions should be of great relevance to the EBRD. The latter is also required, under Article 35, Paragraph 2 of its Agreement, to "report annually on the environmental impact of its activities". The IBRD and IDA, which are not bound by a statutory requirement to this effect, have adopted a similar practice. Their first joint annual report on the environment is being prepared for submission in 1990 to their Executive Directors (and to the Development Committee of the IBRD and IMF Boards of Governors).

iii. Cooperation with other Agencies

Like the charters of other MDBs, the EBRD Agreement includes provisions calling for close cooperation with other agencies, but, unlike them, it places its provision on this matter in the Article dealing with the bank's functions. The ADB Articles specifically refer to cooperation "with the United Nations, its organs and subsidiary bodies including, in particular, the Economic Commission for Asia and the Far East, and with public international organizations, and other international institutions" (Article 2); the IBRD Articles' reference is more general (Article V (8)), as is the IDB provision (Article 2(b)) and that of the AfDB (Article 2(2)). The EBRD Agreement, adopting the more detailed approach, states in Article 2, Paragraph 2 that, in carrying out its functions, it shall work closely with the IMF, IBRD, IFC, MIGA and OECD, and shall cooperate with the U.N. and its Specialized Agencies, and other bodies concerned with the economic development of, and investment in, Central and Eastern Europe.

8. Chairman's Report, commenting on Article 2, Paragraph 1 (vii). *See* Appendix V.

II. MODES AND CONDITIONS OF OPERATION

1. Types of Operation: "Ordinary" and "Special" Operations

The operations of the EBRD are classified into two types, *"ordinary operations"* and *"special operations"*, depending on their source of financing. According to Article 9 of the EBRD Agreement, ordinary operations are those financed from the ordinary capital resources of the bank (enumerated in Article 7), i.e., from (i) the bank's subscribed capital, (ii) its borrowings, (iii) funds received in repayment of loans or guarantees and as proceeds from the disposal of equity investment when such loans, guarantees or investment are financed from the above-mentioned sources, (iv) income derived from loans, guarantees and equity investment financed from the above sources and (v) any other income or funds received by the bank which are not Special Funds. Special operations are, on the other hand, those which rely in their financing on Special Funds.[9] The two types of operation are to be kept separate and apart in every respect, although they may be combined in the financing of one project. In addition to their separate treatment in the books of the bank and in its financial statements, special operations are subject to the agreements (with donors) which determine the use of each Special Fund (Article 11, Paragraph 1 (vii)) and to the rules and regulations to be adopted by EBRD's Board of Directors in their respect (Article 18, Paragraph 3). However, such agreements, rules and regulations must always be consistent with the provisions of the EBRD Agreement (Article 18, Paragraphs 2 and 3).

The IDB, ADB and AfDB charters have similar provisions distinguishing between ordinary and special operations,

9. For the definition of Special Fund resources and the conditions applicable to them and to the EBRD's special operations, *see* Chapter One, pp. 32-36 *supra* and pp. 57-60 of this Chapter, *infra*.

except that ADB's "special funds" include, in addition to the special funds financed by external donors, funds financed from the ADB's paid-in capital and set aside for concessional lending purposes.[10]

There is no similar distinction between ordinary and special operations in the Articles of Agreement of IBRD or IDA, although the latter, while a legally separate institution, may be seen as performing the "special operations" function for the low-income members of both institutions. In any event, the practice of the two institutions does include the administration of "trust funds" which are kept in separate accounts. The policies and practices of the IBRD and IDA with respect to such funds have evolved in an ad hoc manner but were recently codified in the form of an operational directive.[11] According to this directive, the term "trust fund" is used to mean a fund held by the IBRD or IDA as administrator under an agreement with an external donor. The principal condition for seeking or accepting a trust fund is that it should be compatible with IBRD/IDA objectives, policies, and modes of operation. The directive lists a number of considerations which should influence the institutions's decision to accept and administer a trust fund. These are that (a) the objective of the trust fund should be consistent with a specific IBRD/IDA objective, (b) the undertaking should be consistent with the country and sector strategy and lending program of the IBRD/IDA, (c) the IBRD/IDA should have the staff resources and technical capacity to administer the fund effectively, and (d) the procedures for procurement of goods and services should be "broadly consistent" with the principles of economy, efficiency and fair competition as outlined in the IBRD/IDA

10. *See* Articles 19 and 20 of the ADB Articles Agreement, Articles III (3) and IV of IDB's, and Articles 8-11 of AfDB's. *See* also Chapter One, note 27, p.35 *supra.*

11. *See* World Bank, Operational Manual Statement No. 4.40 (Trust Funds), issued in March 1988.

guidelines for procurement and for the use of consultants.

Within this framework, the IBRD and IDA accept and administer a large number of trust funds which broadly fall into two categories: (a) funds which cofinance IBRD/IDA projects or programs (cofinancing trust funds), and (b) funds which are not directly tied to IBRD/IDA loans but which augment or diversify the sources of funding for a wide range of activities including studies, institutional development, training and technical assistance (technical assistance trust funds). At present, the IBRD and IDA administer some 730 active trust funds of both types with a total disbursement exceeding $510 million in fiscal year 1990. In addition to the trust funds administered under the framework of the above-mentioned directive, the IBRD and IDA also accept and administer about 25 "consultant trust funds" under which the donors (mostly bilateral sources) have provided funds to finance the services of short-term consultants to be used for IBRD/IDA operational work.

2. Operating Principles

i. General

The EBRD's operating principles, as stated in Article 13 of its Agreement, are:

(i) The EBRD shall apply sound banking principles to all its operations.[12] There is a similar provision for the ADB (Article 14(xiv)) and AfDB (Article 17(1)(j)); no similar provision exists for the IBRD, but the principle is implied in several provisions and is generally followed in practice.

12. The comment of the Chairman's Report on Article 13(i) suggests that sound banking practices would apply to all the bank's activities, including its financial policies.

(ii) The EBRD shall finance specific projects, whether individual projects or in the context of specific investment programs. This would clearly exclude fast disbursing policy-based lending, as confirmed in the Chairman's Report.[13]

In the IBRD, the Articles of Agreement provide that loans shall be for the purpose of specific projects of reconstruction or development "except in special circumstances" (Article III(4)(vii)). The term "specific project" has been interpreted by the IBRD General Counsel to cover broadly financing for any specific productive purpose.[14] The IDA and the AfDB charters also provide for specific project financing "except in special circumstances" (IDA Article V(1)(b); AfDB Article 17(1)(a)). The IDB's loans are required to be "principally" for specific projects, with an apparent exception for projects under development programs and on-lending for smaller projects (Article III(7)(a)(vi)); the ADB provision is similar to that of the IDB (Article 14(i)).[15]

(iii) The EBRD shall not finance an undertaking in the territory of a member if that member objects. The charters of the IFC (Article III(3)(ii)), MIGA (Article 15), ADB (Article 14(iii)), IDB (Article III(7)(b)) and AfDB (Article 17(1)(b)) have similar restrictions. In the IBRD and IDA, the involvement of the member in whose territory the project is located is stronger in fact; if the member is not the borrower, it has to be involved as the guarantor. In either case, a representative of the Governor of that member is included in the "statutory committee" which recommends the project for approval. The different provision in the EBRD Agree-

13. *See* the Chairman's Report comment on Article 13(ii), Appendix V.

14. *See* Memorandum of the Vice President and General Counsel (Shihata), *Project and Non-Project Financing under the IBRD Articles*, SecM84-19053, December 21, 1984.

15. Lending for other than specific projects in special circumstances was confirmed through a formal interpretation of Article III(4) (vii) of the IBRD charter by the Executive Directors in 1946 and is expressed at present mostly in the form of quick disbursing adjustment loans.

ment, like that in the charters of IFC and MIGA, is explained by its mandate in support of private sector activity.

(iv) The EBRD must not allow a disproportionate amount of its resources to be used for the benefit of any member. This issue is dealt with in a specific manner in Paragraph 3 of Article 11 of the EBRD Agreement. A similar provision exists in ADB's charter (Article 14(xii)) and in the MIGA Convention (Article 22(b)(ii)). No similar provision exists for IBRD, IFC, IDB, or AfDB, but the principle is followed in their operational guidelines and practices.

(v) The EBRD shall seek to maintain reasonable diversification in all its investments. A similar provision is found in the IFC Articles (Article III(3)(vii)). There are also similar provisions, relating to equity investments only, in the charters of the ADB (Article 14, (xiii)) and the AfDB (Article 17(1)(i)). No such provisions appear in the Articles of IBRD, IDA or IDB. There is however a somewhat comparable portfolio diversification provision in MIGA's charter (Article 22(b)(ii)), and in the investment guidelines issued by the Boards of other institutions.

(vi) Before a loan, guarantee or equity investment is granted, the applicant shall have submitted an adequate proposal, and the President shall have presented a written report to the Board regarding the proposal, together with recommendations, on the basis of a staff study. Similar provisions can be found in the charters of ADB (Article 14(iv)), IDB (Article 3(7)(a)(i)) and in the practice of IBRD and its affiliates. As already mentioned, the Articles of Agreement of IBRD and IDA further specifically require that a committee of experts, including a representative of the governor of the member in whose territories the project is located, must submit a report recommending the project for financing.[16]

(vii) The EBRD is meant to be a lender of last resort in the sense that it is prohibited from undertaking any financing or providing any facilities when these can be obtained elsewhere on reasonable terms. Similar provisions can be found in the charters of the IBRD (Article III(4)(i)), IDA (Article V(1)(c)), IFC (Article III(3)(i)), ADB (Article 14(v)), IDB (Article III(7)(a)(ii)) and AfDB (Article 17(1)(c)). These provisions have been liberally understood in practice, however. IDA's Articles prohibit it from extending financing which could be provided by " a loan of the type made by" the IBRD, but this has not precluded the co-financing of the same project by both IBRD and IDA. According to the Chairman's Report, the intention behind the text in the EBRD Agreement, was that "the Bank should not compete with other organizations, rather it should complement or supplement existing financing possibilities".[17]

(viii) Provision of financing or guarantees is preconditioned on the prospective ability of the borrower or guarantor to meet its obligations under the financing contract. Similar provisions can be found in the charters of IBRD (Article III (4)(v)), ADB (Article 14(vi)), IDB (Article III(7)(a)) (iii)), and AfDB (Article 17(1)(e)). These provisions require the bank concerned "to pay due regard to the *prospects"* that the borrower and its guarantor, if any, *"will* be in a position to meet its obligations..." under each loan or guarantee (emphasis

16. The IBRD General Counsel took the position in 1969 that, with respect to loan proposals "no decision which departs materially from the President's recommendations and those of the Statutory Committee, should be taken by the Executive Directors unless and until such a new proposal has been considered by the Statutory Committee in question and has been recommended by it and the President to the Executive Directors". *See* Memorandum of the General Counsel (Broches), *Board Procedure Relating to Loan and Credit Proposals*, SecM69-12, March 17, 1969.

17. Chairman's Report comment on Article 13(vii), *see* Appendix V.

added). In the IBRD's practice, this has been translated into a general creditworthiness requirement which, if not met, disqualifies the member from borrowing from IBRD. Such a disqualification does not by itself qualify the member of both institutions for borrowing from IDA where it has to meet all IDA's eligibility requirements.

(ix) Disbursements of loans are to be made for meeting expenditure as they are actually incurred. Similar provisions can be found in the charters of IBRD (Article III(5)(c)), IDA (Article V(1)(h)), ADB (Article 14(x)), and AfDB (Article 17(1)(g)). The practice of these institutions includes under these provisions "retroactive financing" within certain limits and the IBRD and IDA have allowed in recent years advance disbursement to "special accounts" opened by the borrowers under specific requirements.

(x) The EBRD shall seek to revolve its funds by selling its investments whenever it can do so on satisfactory terms. The term "investments" in this respect includes, according to the Chairman's Report, both loans and guarantees and equity investments. Fostering the local capital market should be borne in mind in choosing the investment to be sold, according to the same source.

(xi) Terms and conditions for investments should be appropriate, taking into account the requirements of the enterprise, risks for the EBRD and private investors' terms and conditions for similar financing. Provisions in the IBRD, ADB, IDB and AfDB charters refer only to "suitable compensation" when guaranteeing a loan made by other investors. [18]

(xii) The EBRD places no restriction upon procurement of goods and services *from any country*, for both ordinary and special operations, but require procurements to be based when appropriate on international bidding. No similar requirement is followed in the IFC. The IBRD

18. *See* IBRD, Article III(4) (vi); IDB, Article III(7)(a)(v); ADB, Article 14(viii); AfDB, Article 17(1)(k).

rules generally require international competitive bidding but limit procurement to member countries (with minor exceptions). Tied procurement has been accepted in IBRD and IDA under some trust funds in recent years, as will soon be shown.

(xiii) The proceeds of any loan, guarantee or equity participation shall be used only for the purposes for which it was granted, and with due attention to considerations of economy and efficiency. This provision is similar to those of the IBRD, IDA, ADB, IDB and AfDB, except that the charters of these institutions add language to the effect that this would occur without regard to political or other non-economic influences or considerations.

ii. Procurement Principles

As mentioned earlier, the EBRD Agreement provides for completely open procurement of the goods and services financed, that is for procurement from the territories of members and non members alike. This explicitly applies to both ordinary and special operations. Furthermore, "in all appropriate cases, [the EBRD shall] make its loans and other operations conditional on international invitation to tender being arranged" (Article 13(xii)). Such tenders should, according to the Chairman's Report, be "genuinely competitive, in line with the G.A.T.T. Agreement on Government Procurement". This may indicate a departure from the preference given to local contractors and suppliers under the procurement guidelines of other MDBs inasmuch as the G.A.T.T. Agreement on Government Procurement stipulates for non-discrimination between foreign and local suppliers.[19] The Chairman's Report makes two additional

19. *See* G.A.T.T. Agreement on Government Procurement, April 12, 1979, at Article II(1). However, it appears that developing countries may under the special and differential treatment accorded to them in Article III of the G.A.T.T. Agreement on Government Procurement give preference to local suppliers. Countries such as Yugoslavia have been treated as developing countries in UNCTAD and other contexts.

points: "Private sector enterprises in which the Bank held equity or debt might be encouraged, but not obliged, to use international tenders to obtain goods or services efficiently and economically."[20] This is the practice of IFC. By contrast, in the IBRD for example, private borrowers, like public ones, are required to follow the IBRD's procurement guidelines, which as a general rule require international competitive bidding for all but small contracts. The second additional point made by the Chairman's Report on the EBRD Agreement is that open procurement from non member countries has been meant as an "original gesture", "to give less developed countries, who might not become members, the opportunity to tender for Bank contracts".[21]

Under the IBRD and IDA Articles, neither of these institutions can restrict procurement to any given country. The procurement guidelines applicable to their loans, but not the Articles of Agreement, limit procurement to member countries but allow procurement from Switzerland (as agreed with the latter) and from Taiwan, China (as arranged at the time the People's Republic of China assumed representation of China in the IBRD). In the ADB, as a general rule, procurement is limited to member countries, but an exception is allowed in the Articles (Article 14(ix)) in any case where the Board of Directors so decides by a special majority provided this is done "in special circumstances". A similar provision exists in the AfDB charter (Article 17(1)(d)).

The extension of the principle of open procurement to EBRD's special operations where tied funds are not allowed is a welcome addition in the EBRD Agreement. It provides

20. *See* also EBRD Article 13(xii), which requires international invitations to tender "in all *appropriate* cases" (emphasis added).

21. *See* Chairman's Report comments on Article 13 (xii) where it adds that this gesture is meant to reassure these less developed countries "that the interest of shareholders in the new Bank did not mean reduced interest in their traditional partners in development."

a clear signal to the donor community that the EBRD legally cannot and therefore will not accept or administer funds which dilute its multilateral character or impose terms and conditions which are in conflict with the relevant provisions of the EBRD Agreement.

In practice, the ADB (which was established in 1966) has since the early seventies refused to accept or administer funds tied to procurement restrictions or subject to other terms and conditions in conflict with the relevant parallel provisions of the ADB Agreement.

As indicated earlier, procurement for goods and services under the "cofinancing" and "technical assistance" trust funds administered by the IBRD and IDA should, in accordance with the IBRD/IDA directive on such funds, be generally consistent with the principles of economy, efficiency and fair competition embodied in the principles applicable to procurement under those institutions' loans. However, the IBRD management has recently provided some flexibility in accepting tied trust funds along the above-mentioned lines, under ad hoc cofinancing and technical assistance trust fund agreements but has indicated that every effort should be made to convince donors to untie either all or a portion of their trust funds. Under the terms of the existing cofinancing *framework* agreements of IBRD and IDA with various cofinanciers, the IBRD and IDA continue to maintain the position that they will not accept or administer tied cofinancing funds; where cofinancing funds are provided on a tied basis, *parallel* cofinancing arrangements are entered into and the cofinancier administers its own funds, signs its own agreements with the borrower and supervises procurement financed by its funds. As for the "consultant trust funds" accepted and administered by the IBRD and IDA, these are usually provided on a tied basis, i.e. tied to the engagement of consultants from the donor country. The stated rationale for the administration of such tied funds by the IBRD and IDA is that they constitute a multi-donor pool of funds and the administrator is thus free to choose and finance consultants on a reasonably competitive basis from the approximately 25 countries funding the pool.

The open procurement principle of the EBRD is consistent with the growing trend towards liberalization of international trade. It is expected to be elaborated upon in detailed guidelines to be approved by EBRD's Board of Directors. Such guidelines may further be expected to reflect a broader outlook than that contained in the IBRD/IDA guidelines.

3. Methods of Operation

The EBRD may carry out its operations in several ways, but seems to be limited to certain operating methods which are enumerated as follows in Article 11:[22]

(i) making, or co-financing with multilateral institutions, commercial banks or other interested sources, loans to (a) private enterprises, (b) state-owned enterprises operating competitively (defined in the Article as operating autonomously in a competitive market environment and subject to bankruptcy laws) and moving to participation in a market-oriented economy, and (c) state-owned enterprises to facilitate their transition to private ownership and control and in particular to "facilitate or enhance the participation of private and/or foreign capital in such enterprises". The word "domestic" seems to have been missed after the word "private" in the last-quoted phrase but may readily be assumed;

(ii) investment in the equity capital of private sector enterprises, state-owned enterprises operating competitively and state-owned enterprises to facilitate tran-

22. Article 11 states that "[t]he Bank *shall* carry out its operations... in any or all of the following ways" (emphasis added). The comment on this provision in the Chairman's Report further states that "[t]he Article establishes the ways the Bank shall carry out its purpose and functions...".

sition to private ownership and control and, where other means of financing are not appropriate, underwriting the equity issue of securities by both private and state-owned enterprises which meet the criteria described above;

(iii) provision of guarantees to facilitate access to domestic and international capital markets by both private and state-owned enterprises described above;

(iv) deploying Special Fund resources in accordance with the agreements determining their use; and

(v) making or participating in loans and providing technical assistance for the reconstruction or development of infrastructure "including environmental programs, *necessary* for private sector development and the transition to a market-oriented economy" (emphasis added).

While the EBRD shares with all other MDBs the main function of providing, and guaranteeing, loans, the EBRD Agreement emphasizes certain types of recipients and purposes. The EBRD's main potential recipients are private sector enterprises and state-owned enterprises meeting certain criteria; the main methods of operations being direct loans, guarantees of loans or investment in the enterprises' equity capital. Equity participations are not authorized for the IBRD, although they were envisaged early in the preparation of its Articles and reference to "other investment" (than loans and guarantees) survived, without consequence, in its Article I. In this respect the EBRD is, to a large extent, closer to the IFC which, following the amendment of its Articles in 1961, is broadly authorized to invest its funds "in such form or forms as it may deem appropriate in the circumstances" (Article III(2)).

Direct loans *to member countries* for investment projects, which have been the main business of other MDs, are less emphasized in the EBRD Agreement, and are listed as the last method of operation, confined to infrastructure, including environment programs, lumped together with technical assistance and conditional on being necessary for private sector development and the transition to a market-oriented economy.

The general methods of operations enumerated above are likely to be elaborated on in operating policy statements to be adopted by the Board of Directors.[23] In the IBRD and IDA, specific operating policies and requirements can be found in several Board decisions, management operational directives and in the "General Conditions Applicable to Loan and Guarantee Agreements". The latter conditions are incorporated by reference into each loan agreement and are therefore binding on the IBRD/IDA and their borrowers.

The Board of Directors of the EBRD is further given the authority to review, at least annually, EBRD operations and lending strategy in each recipient country to ensure that the purpose and functions of the EBRD are fully served (Article 11, Paragraph 2). Decisions pursuant to such review, which presumably may involve discussion of both the bank's operations strategy for the country and its own performance under such operations, can be taken only by a majority of not less than two thirds of the Directors representing not less than three fourths of the total voting power. In IDA's current practice, more extensive "country discussions" may take place on the first occasion in the fiscal year of considering an adjustment loan for the country or, in the absence of such form of lending to the country concerned, on the first occasion of an investment loan. The same practice seems to be increasingly followed for IBRD operations in spite of some controversy about its appropriateness.

23. The Chairman's Report, in its comments on Article 13, anticipates this for the operating principles mentioned in that Article. The experience of the IBRD and other MDBs shows that operational directives cover detailed issues related to both operating principles and methods.

4. Terms and Conditions for Loans and Guarantees

i. General

The EBRD is required to take full account of the need to safeguard its income in setting terms and conditions for its financing operations (Article 14, Paragraph 1). Term-setting provisions for the other institutions do not emphasize the need to safeguard income. According to the Chairman's Report, the delegates meant the requirement of safeguarding EBRD's income to "avoid the risk of [its] operations being in practice subsidized from the cost-free resources available to the Bank from members' paid-in subscriptions". Such a risk is avoided in the IBRD at present by determining the interest rate on its loans according to the cost of its borrowings (plus one half of one percent) regardless of how the particular loan is financed.

Where the recipient of loans or guarantees is not itself a member, but a state-owned enterprise, the requirement for a guarantee is more flexible in the case of the EBRD (Article 14, Paragraph 2 which is similar to Article 15(2) ADB) than in the case of the IBRD. The EBRD provision permits the Board of Directors to consider a wide range of factors in deciding a policy on guarantees for loans to such state-enterprises. A guarantee *may,* but does not have to be required from the member or members in whose territory the project is to be carried out, or from a public agency or any instrumentality of that member or those members acceptable to the EBRD. By contrast, the IBRD charter (Article III(4)(i)) requires a guarantee from the member in whose territories the project is located in every case where the borrower is not the member itself.

It should be noted that the optional guarantee provided for in Article 14 of the EBRD Agreement is limited to loans to state enterprises and does not apply therefore to loans to private enterprises. This is consistent with the requirements of IFC Articles and is confirmed in the Chairman's Report's comment on Article 14 of the EBRD Agreement where emphasis is placed on the "fundamental goal" of developing a strong private sector. To this end, the Report explicitly states that:

> "To ensure that private entrepreneurs took full responsibility for their commercial undertakings, the Board shall follow the present practice of the International Finance Corporation in not requiring a member government guarantee on loans to private sector enterprises".[24]

Furthermore, the Report seems to encourage EBRD not to require state guarantees even for loans to public sector enterprises. The EBRD, according to the comment of the Chairman's Report on Article 14, "could take into account the fact that a state-owned enterprise would be more likely to respond quickly to market forces, and to make the transition to market-oriented economies, if that enterprise could not rely on a government guarantee to discharge its responsibilities under a Bank loan". Variant loan terms could then compensate EBRD for the risks of not having such guarantee, as the Report suggests.

Also according to the Chairman's Report, when the EBRD requires a member country guarantee for a loan to a state-owned enterprise (i.e. guarantee by the member or a public agency or instrumentality) the loan shall be considered as made to the state sector, unless the state-owned enterprise is in transition to private ownership and control. A former state-owned enterprise which has achieved private ownership and control will be regarded as a private sector enterprise, and the EBRD will not require member country guarantees on new loans to that enterprise.

24. The IFC practice referred to in the above comment is based on Article I of the IFC Articles which provides that it "shall.. assist in financing... productive private enterprises... without guarantee of repayment by the member government concerned."

ii. Interest, Commissions and Fees

The EBRD's charges on loans made as part of the ordinary operations will include interest, commissions on loans, and guarantee fees. Article 14 does not specifically require that the interest rate applicable to EBRD loans be decided by the Board of Directors, although this is required in Article 15 for the determination of commissions and guarantee fees. This differentiation does not seem to be justified and the Board may be expected to adopt a formula for determining the applicable interest rate or rates, which is not a less significant matter than determining commissions. "Interest rate policy" is indeed listed in the Chairman's Report comments on Article 29 among the "general policy decisions" which require Board approval by a special majority. In addition, the Board may decide any other charges on the ordinary operations, and any commissions, fees or other charges in its Special Funds operations (Article 15). These provisions are similar to those of the ADB and AfDB charters (except for the details of computing the commission).[25]

The IBRD Articles also deal with payment provisions, and stipulate that the terms and conditions of interest and amortization payments, maturity and dates of payments of each loan shall be determined by the IBRD, together with the rate and any other terms and conditions of commission to be charged in connection with the loan (Article IV(4)). This provision includes a number of details regarding the manner of computing commission during the first ten years, and after that, taking into account the reserve situation of IBRD. The details of applicable interest, commission and fees appear in the text of the IBRD's loan agreements. The same is required by Article 14, Paragraph 1 of the EBRD Agreement.

25. *See* ADB, Article 16; AfDB, Article 19.

5. Limitations on Operations

i. General Limit

For the EBRD, as for most other MDBs, "The total amount of outstanding loans, equity investments and guarantees made by the Bank in the ordinary operations shall not be increased at any time, if by such increase the total amount of its unimpaired subscribed capital, reserves and surpluses included in its ordinary capital resources would be exceeded" (Article 12, Paragraph 1). [26]

It is unfortunate that the EBRD Agreement used this language which has caused confusion in the practice of other institutions. The text appears in the IBRD Articles under a conflicting heading which refers to limitation on *borrowings* and guarantees. The drafting history of this provision in the IBRD Articles also suggests that what the drafters had in mind was to place a general limit on the IBRD's obligations rather than on its assets at risk. However, the text clearly covers loans and guarantees (as well as equity investment in the case of EBRD) which, for disbursed loans and equity investments, are assets and not liabilities. In the IBRD, the limit has always been understood in practice to refer to the disbursed and not yet repaid amount of loans. This is also the present understanding in IDB. In the ADB, however, the same text is understood to cover all

26. *See* also IBRD Article III (3); ADB Article 12 (1); IDB, Article III (5) (a); AfDb, Article 15, (1). There are two necessary differences between the EBRD text and that of the IBRD. The IBRD's Article III (3) does not include equity investments since the IBRD does not finance such investments. Nor is there a reference in the IBRD text to "ordinary operations" as there is no distinction in the IBRD between ordinary and special operations. It is clear, however, that loans financed by trust funds are not included in the IBRD lending limit. It may also be noted that the counterpart provision of the IFC Articles (Article III(6) (i)) imposes only a temporary restriction in this respect on the level of IFC financing operations (the restriction is to apply only "if and so long as the Corporation shall be indebted on loans from or guaranteed by" the IBRD). Also, the IFC limit, unlike that of the other banks including EBRD takes the form of a debt/equity ratio.

committed loans, regardless of disbursements. In theory, the text could also be read to mean the undisbursed amounts of committed loans as only these represent obligations to borrowers under the bank's loans. The confusion extends to the meaning of the total amount outstanding of guarantees which, given the IBRD's understanding of what "outstanding loans" mean, has been interpreted in the IBRD's practice to mean only the callable amounts of guarantees.[27] This confusion could have certainly been avoided by a clearer text for the EBRD. Instead, the IBRD provision was repeated *verbatim* (with the necessary editorial additions mentioned earlier). The Chairman's Report provides guidance, however, in its comment on Article 12, Paragraph 1. It states that the delegates "shared the view that the Board of Directors should exercise prudence in approving all such *commitments* in line with its obligations under paragraph 1 of this Article" (emphasis added). This may suggest an interpretation similar to that followed in the ADB or it may only require a great measure of caution in adopting a broader interpretation.

ii. Limit on Loans, Guarantees and Equity Investments for the State Sector

According to Article 11, Paragraph 3 of the EBRD Agreement "[n]ot more than forty (40) percent of the amount of the Bank's total committed loans, guarantees and equity investments... shall be provided to the state sector. Such percentage limit shall apply initially over a two (2) year period, from the date of commencement of the Bank's operations, taking one year with another, and thereafter in respect of each subsequent financial year". This clear limitation is without prejudice, however, to the other operations

27. *See* for a detailed account, Memorandum of the IBRD Vice President and General Counsel (Shihata), *The IBRD Lending Limit. Legal Analysis of the Requirements of Article III, Section 3 of the IBRD Articles of Agreement* (R87, January 13, 1987, Annex 6).

referred to in Article 11, i.e., it does not apply to technical assistance through means other than loans and guarantees or equity participation, *underwriting* the equity issue of securities by beneficiary enterprises which does not entail an actual equity investment by EBRD, financial advice and other form of assistance to facilitate access of enterprises to capital markets, as well as, one assumes, special operations financed by Special Funds under the conditions agreed with their respective donors.

A similar limit applies, furthermore, to loans, guarantees and equity investments for each recipient country. Not more than 40% of the total amount committed in the three above-mentioned forms of operations is to be provided to the state sector of any country over a period of five years (taking one year with another). As the previous limit, this one does not apply to the other forms of operations listed earlier (Article 11, Paragraph 3 (ii)).

Neither limit applies, however, to (a) financial assistance to a state-owned enterprise which is implementing a program to achieve private ownership and control, and (b) loans to financial intermediaries for on-lending to the private sector (Article 11, Paragraph 3 (iii)).

The state sector is defined for the purpose of the two limits mentioned above to include "national and local governments, their agencies, and enterprises owned or controlled by any of them".

iii. Limits on Equity Investments

Two limits on equity investments appear in the EBRD Agreement. The first is a general limit which explicitly applies to "disbursed equity investment," defined, in the Chairman's Report, as "excluding any such investments as might subsequently have been disposed of ". Such disbursed equity investment "shall not at any time exceed an amount corresponding to [the EBRD's] total unimpaired *paid-in* subscribed capital, surpluses and general reserve" (Article 12, Paragraph 3) (emphasis added). The limit is related to the paid-in capital and thus differs from the more general limit applicable to the total amount of outstanding loans, guarantees and equity investments which is related to all the unimpaired subscribed capital, i.e. to the full subscribed capital net of losses. Furthermore, the more specific limit explicitly applies to *disbursed* equity investment and not to all amounts committed for this purpose. In the ADB and the AfDB, a comparable limit is imposed by Articles 12(3) and 15(4)(a) respectively on the order of 10% of paid-in capital, surplus and reserves, and applies to "outstanding" investments which, presumably, means also disbursed investments net of investments already disposed of.

The second limit on equity investment relates to the equity capital of the enterprise receiving the investment (rather than to the EBRD's capital resources). The Board of Directors is vested with the authority to make a general rule stipulating the maximum stake that the EBRD can take in the equity of any enterprise (Article 12, Paragraph 2), again as is the case in the AfDB (Article 15(4)(b)). In the ADB, a 10% limit of the paid in capital is specified in the Articles (Article 12(3)) for the same purpose. As under a somewhat similar provision in the IFC Articles (Article III(3)(iv) as amended) the EBRD may not seek to obtain by such an investment a controlling interest in the enterprise concerned, nor may it exercise such control to assume direct responsibility for managing such enterprise, except in the event of actual or threatened default or insolvency, or other situations which the EBRD judges as threatening such an investment. A similar clause also exists in the Articles of ADB (Article 12(4)) and AfDB (Article 15(4)(b)), except that these clauses do not specify the instances in which the institution may seek control of, or assume responsibility for managing the entity concerned. In the ADB, the exception is stipulated in general terms "where necessary to safeguard the investment of ADB."

iv. Prohibition of Guarantees of Export Credits and Insurance Activities

Article 12, Paragraph 4 of the EBRD Agreement contains a flat prohibition of "guarantees for export credits" and "insurance activities." This clause clearly means that EBRD is not allowed to compete with the national agencies (public and private) which provide these services, nor with MIGA (as far as investment insurance against non commercial risks is involved). A narrower prohibition regarding export credits only is included in MIGA's Operational Regulations for the same purpose.[28]

v. Limit on Operations in a Member Requesting Access to Resources for a Limited Period and Purposes (Operations in the Soviet Union)

The EBRD Agreement has a unique provision which seems to be intended to apply only to the Soviet Union, although it is drafted in general terms, and clearly represents a compromise solution. The Soviet Union, it should be noted, is not yet in a state of transition towards multiparty democracy, pluralism, or a market economy, but strong indications suggest that it is moving in this direction. Its economy is also much larger than those of all the other Central and Eastern European countries combined. As drafted, the provision under discussion (Article 8, Paragraph 4) simply gives any potential recipient country the option to request that the EBRD provide access to its resources for limited purposes, over a period of three years beginning after entry into force of the EBRD Agreement. Such a request is to be attached to the Agreement as an integral part of it. The request has been made in fact by the Soviet Union only, whose letter to this effect is now attached to the Agreement.

A number of conditions are attached to EBRD activities benefitting the requesting member in such a case. First, the

28. *See* Shihata, *MIGA and Foreign Investment* 114-15 (1988).

financing shall be in the form of technical assistance, or other types of assistance, to facilitate the transition of state-owned enterprises to private sector ownership and control, subject to the 40% restriction described under "Limit on Loans, Guarantees and Equity Investments for the State Sector" above. Second, the total amount of assistance provided shall not exceed the total amount of cash disbursed and promissory notes issued by the requesting country for its shares. Third, any decision to allow such a country access beyond the time and amounts specified above shall be taken by the Board of Governors by the exceptional majority of not less than three fourths of the Governors representing not less than eighty-five percent of the voting power.

The provision of Article 8, Paragraph 4 uses in this context the phrase "limited purposes," which is defined in the Article as "...technical assistance and other types of assistance directed to finance its private sector, to facilitate transition of state-owned enterprises to private ownership...". It is interesting therefore to note that technical assistance which normally accounts for a small portion of the activities of other MDBs and possibly of the EBRD itself is mentioned in this particular context as if it would be the main form of operations for the requesting country, while investment loans, guarantees and participations, which are also included, are referred to merely as "other types of [eligible] assistance".

It should be noted that in his requesting letter, submitted to the Chairman of the Conference which approved the Agreement, the head of the Soviet delegation seems to have based his country's request, formulated as an intent or preparedness to limit its access, only on the proposition that "certain difficulties largely stem from fears of a number of countries that due to the size of its economy the Soviet Union may become the principal recipient of credits of the Bank and therefore will narrow its capacity to extend aid to other Central and Eastern European Countries". The letter further explains that the Soviet Union's intentions to become a member of EBRD "account primarily for its will to establish a new institution of multilateral co-operation so as to foster historical reforms on the European continent." The letter nevertheless expresses confidence that "continuing economic reforms in the Soviet Union will inevitably promote the expansion of the Bank's activities into the territory of the Soviet Union." However, it tempers this expectation by stating that the USSR, "being interested in securing the multilateral character of the Bank, will not choose that at any time in future the Soviet borrowings will exceed an amount consistent with maintaining the necessary diversity in the bank's operations and prudent limits on its exposure".

6. Methods of Meeting Liabilities

The EBRD is empowered to take such action as it deems appropriate to deal, in its ordinary operations, with arrears or default on loans made, participated in or guaranteed by EBRD, and in cases of losses on underwritings and in equity investments (Article 17). EBRD is also required to maintain adequate provisions against possible losses, and to charge such losses, in the following order, to: (i) provisions against losses; (ii) net income; (iii) special reserve; (iv) general reserve and surplus; (v) unimpaired paid-in capital; and (vi) an appropriate amount of the uncalled subscribed callable capital (Article 17). It is worth noting that these provisions relate only to losses arising in ordinary operations. As indicated earlier in Chapter One,[29] no provision is made by EBRD in respect of possible losses arising in special operations. This matter is expected to be arranged with the sources of the Special Funds financing such operations.

29. *See* Chapter One, p.35 *supra.*

The Articles of Agreement of the IBRD (Article IV(7)) and of the ADB (Article 18) deal with the problems arising from borrowers' default in a different order. Both institutions are empowered to take such action as they deem appropriate to adjust the obligations of borrowers under their loans. This matter is separate, however, from the issue of charging losses which are to be charged, in the following order, to: (i) special reserve; (ii) other reserves, surplus and available paid-in capital; and (iii) uncalled subscribed callable capital. Beyond that, the IBRD Articles contain detailed provisions which were meant to apply when a borrower member suffers from "an acute exchange stringency". The IBRD is authorized in such cases and before default actually occurs to accept repayment in the borrower's local currency, subject to a repurchase arrangement, or to "modify the terms of amortization or extend the life of the loan, or both" (Article IV(4)(c)). If the borrower actually defaults, the IBRD is authorized to relax conditions of loan service in the same manner or otherwise under certain conditions.[30] The IBRD has not however followed the options provided in these provisions since the 1960s and the EBRD Agreement avoids similar provisions in its text.

The EBRD Agreement further requires that each loan or guarantee agreement shall expressly state the currency or currencies or ECU for all payments due under it (Article 14, Paragraph 3). Except for the reference to ECU, this provision is similar to those of ADB (Article 15(3)), IDB (Article III(10)(b)) and AfDB (Article 18(3)(c)). The IBRD provision (Article IV(4)(b)) also requires that the currency or currencies of payment be specified. However, it goes on to require repayment of the actual "currency loaned" for loans made out of its own funds and to limit the overall amount outstanding in a particular currency for loans made

30. For details *see* Memorandum of the IBRD Vice President and General Counsel (Shihata), *Treatment of Bank Borrowers in Cases of "Acute Exchange Stringencies" and "Default"*, SecM86-660/1, June 18, 1986.

out of borrowed funds to those borrowed by IBRD in the same currency. Repayment of the "currency loaned" for ordinary operations is also required for the ADB (Article 15(1)) and AfDB (Article 18(2)(b)). In the IBRD, the restrictions imposed by these provisions have been broadly accommodated in its currency management practice which now operates in a manner different from, though not inconsistent with that envisaged in the Articles.[31] Without similar provisions, which the EBRD Agreement wisely avoids, the EBRD is likely to have greater latitude in designing its currency management practices.

The IBRD Articles also have a specific text on the provision of currencies for direct loans (Article IV(3)), which has no parallel in the EBRD Agreement. These IBRD provisions restrict financing of local expenditures to rather limited and exceptional circumstances.[32] These provisions, however, have proved impractical in practice and the EBRD Agreement appropriately avoids them.

III. SUSPENSION AND TERMINATION OF OPERATIONS

Like other MDBs, the EBRD is established for an unlimited period, but provisions are made for the possible suspension or termination of its operations. The EBRD Agreement follows in this respect the almost standard texts of the Articles of the IBRD (Article VI(5)), IFC (Article V(5)), IDB (Article X), ADB (Articles 44-46) and AfDB (Article 46-48).

31. *See* Memorandum of the IBRD Legal Department, *Legal and Policy Restrictions in the Borrowing, Use and Conversion of Currencies by the Bank*, SecM88-272, March 14, 1988.

32. *See* Memorandum by the General Counsel (Broches), *Foreign Exchange Loans for Local Expenditures*, SecM68-436, November 29, 1968.

None of these provisions has ever been applied in practice.[33]

In an emergency situation, not defined in the Agreement, the Board of Directors of the EBRD may suspend temporarily new operations "pending an opportunity for further consideration and action by the *Board of Governors* " (Article 40) (emphasis added). The latter Board may presumably lift the suspension or continue it by a simple majority. It may also decide, by a special majority of not less than two thirds of the Governors representing not less than three fourths of the total voting power of the members, to terminate the bank's operations. Such termination of operations entails the cessation of all the bank's activities, "except those incident to the orderly realization, conservation and preservation of its assets and settlement of its obligations" (Article 41).

A decision to terminate the Bank's operations does *not* immediately terminate the members' liability for callable subscriptions to the capital. Such liability continues for the uncalled subscriptions "until all claims of creditors, including all contingent claims, shall have been discharged". The EBRD outstanding obligations, including those arising under its guarantees (contingent claims), would continue in effect unless provided otherwise in the debt or guarantee instrument (Article 42, Paragraph 1). The Agreement clarifies how the "direct claims" of "creditors on ordinary operations" would be paid. Under Article 42, Paragraph 2 , such claims shall be paid *first* out of the assets of the bank,

33. It may be argued that the special purpose of EBRD which supports the transition to open market-oriented economies may justify termination of its operations once this transition has been completed and thus that the provisions of the EBRD Agreement on such termination stand a greater chance of application than in other MDBs. It should be noted, however, that the EBRD purpose includes as well the promotion of private and entrepreneurial initiative in the recipient countries which apply specified principles (*see* pp. 41-48 *supra*) and that this would make it as much of an on-going concern as any other MDB and as the IFC in particular.

secondly out of the payments to be made to the bank in respect of unpaid paid-in shares and *lastly* out of payments to the bank in respect of callable shares. It may be assumed however that EBRD will manage its finances so as to obviate the need for any recourse to callable capital, as is the case in the IBRD.

Before making any payments to creditors holding direct claims, the EBRD Board of Directors must first make such arrangements as it may find necessary "to ensure a *pro rata* distribution among holders of direct and holders of contingent claims" (Article 42, Paragraph 2). This provision does not give any priority to either type of claim and may apply in the unlikely event of having liabilities which exceed the bank's capital resources.

Distribution of the EBRD's assets to its members cannot be made before "all liabilities to creditors have been discharged or provided for". Furthermore, such a distribution may be made only by a decision of the Board of Governors acting by a special majority (two thirds of the Governors representing not less than three fourths of the total voting power). Such a distribution, if made, "shall be in proportion to the capital stock held by each member" (Article 43, Paragraph 2). It is assumed that the reference is to the total capital stock and not just the actually paid-in shares. The time and conditions of distribution will be "as the Bank shall deem fair and equitable". At any rate, distributions "need not be uniform as to type of assets" and no member shall be entitled to receive its share of the assets before it settles all its obligations to the bank. The Agreement adds that any member receiving assets distributed in this manner "shall enjoy the same rights with respect to such assets as the Bank enjoyed prior to their distribution" (Article 43, Paragraph 3).

Chapter Three

Organization and Management: Membership; Organizational Structure; Status and Immunities; Interpretation, Amendment and Arbitration

While the organizational structure of EBRD is identical to that of other MDBs, the categorization of its members, its voting provisions and some of the details related to the status and immunities of its officers differ in some important respects from existing arrangements in other institutions. This Chapter deals consecutively with relevant, varied issues which are dealt with under Articles 3, 22 to 32 and 44 to 58 of the EBRD Agreement while comparing them with their counterparts in the charters of other MDBs.

I. MEMBERSHIP

Under Article 3, Paragraph 1, of the EBRD Agreement, membership is open to two categories of countries, which are classified into two groups only, "European countries" and "non European countries which are members of the International Monetary Fund", as well as two specific international organizations (the EEC and the EIB). The term "European", which describes the first group of member countries and appears in the names of the two member organizations, is not defined in the Agreement. However, Annex A to the Agreement, which sets out the initial subscriptions of prospective members, groups them into four categories:

(i) *"Members of the European Communities,"* which include two sub-groups consisting, respectively, of (a) 12 European countries and (b) the EEC and the EIB,

(ii) *"Other European Countries,"* which include 11 countries not all geographically located in continental Europe and one of which (Israel) is not otherwise described in international agencies as a European state,

(iii) *"Recipient Countries,"* which are also referred to elsewhere in the Agreement as "Central and Eastern European Countries," a group consisting of 8 countries, including the Soviet Union, and

(iv) *"Non European Countries,"* which groups together 9 countries not otherwise grouped as a separate category in any international context. These include the largest shareholder in the bank (the U.S.), one of the second largest shareholders (Japan), Canada, Australia and New Zealand, as well as four developing countries (Egypt, Korea, Mexico and Morocco) which will not be recipient countries in the EBRD.

On this basis, the forty original signatory states of the EBRD Agreement, listed in Annex A, would comprise 31 "European countries" (the 12 EEC members, 11 other European countries and 8 recipient countries) and 9 non-European countries.

The provisions of Article 3 on membership are noteworthy in two ways. First, membership of non European Countries (but not that of the European Countries) is conditioned upon membership in the IMF. Among the regional development banks, a requirement that non-regional members be members of the IMF is found in the Articles of Agreement of the IDB. Membership of non-regional countries in the ADB is conditioned upon being a "developed" country and being a member of the U.N. or of any of its specialized agencies. Membership of non-regional states in the AfDB is conditioned on their being members of, or contributors to, the African Development Fund.

Second, two of the members are not states, but international organizations, namely the EEC and the EIB. Membership of international organizations is not permitted by the Articles of Agreement of the World Bank Group organizations and of the regional development banks. However, AfDB is a member of its soft loan affiliate, the African Development Fund.[1]

The EBRD Agreement is to some extent comparable to the Articles of the regional development banks in classifying members on a regional basis. In the regional development banks' Articles, provisions are made to protect the voting power of the "regional" members. The EBRD Agreement contains provisions designed to protect the voting power majority of a sub-group of the "regional" members, namely the members belonging to the EEC plus the EEC itself and the EIB. On the basis of their subscriptions listed in Annex A,[2] these members would hold 51% of the potential initial total voting power. As indicated earlier, under Article 5, Paragraphs 2 and 4 of the EBRD Agreement, no shares may

1. Membership by "any grouping of States" is authorized in the Agreement Establishing the International Fund for Agricultural Development (IFAD) with a view to accommodating in particular possible membership by the European Community, but IFAD's membership remains confined to states.

2. In contrast to the position under the Articles of the other MDBs, voting power in the EBRD is, as mentioned at p. 88 *infra*, exclusively related to subscriptions, with no additional "basic" or "free" membership votes being assigned to members.

be allocated to new or existing members if this would have the effect of reducing the total shares held by the "protected" members below a majority of the total subscribed capital stock, and hence reducing their total voting power below the majority of the total voting power.

These arrangements may also be compared to those made under the MIGA Convention, which classifies members into two groups, Categories One (developed countries) and Two (developing countries) and contains provisions designed to maintain the voting power of one group (the developing member countries) at an initial minimum level (with an attempt to be made subsequently to establish voting parity between the two Categories).[3] The IDA Articles distinguish between "Part I" and "Part II" countries, but this is relevant only for the purpose of payment of initial subscriptions by the original members of the Association;[4] the Articles of the IBRD and IFC contain no similar provisions classifying members or aimed at maintaining the relative voting power of groups of members. However, in the general practice of these agencies, developing countries are often referred to as Part II countries, following the terminology of IDA but not always its classification.[5]

The EBRD Agreement also classifies members for the purpose of eligibility for assistance from the bank, with eight Central and Eastern European Countries being designated as potential "recipients" of such assistance. An analogous approach is taken by the MIGA Convention, which limits the Agency's ordinary guarantee operations to investments made in developing member countries, defined as those listed in the Convention as Category Two members. There are no similar classifications of members in the Articles of the IBRD, IFC and IDA, but the practice of these organiza-

3. *See* Articles 3, 39(a)–(c) and Schedule A of the MIGA Convention.

4. *See* Article II, Section 2(d) of the IDA Articles.

5. Kuwait and the UAE are included in Part I under IDA but are normally included in the informal references to "Part II" in the practices of IBRD and IFC.

tions has developed "graduation policies" under which higher income members are no longer eligible to receive their assistance.

Article 37 of the EBRD Agreement entitles any member to withdraw from the bank by sending a notice to it to this effect. Cessation of membership takes effect on the date specified in the withdrawal notice but in no event less than six months after such notice is received by the bank. Similar provisions are found in the Articles of the regional development banks and in the MIGA Convention, except that in MIGA the "waiting period" between serving a withdrawal notice and its effectiveness (a period during which the member can revoke the notice) is three months, rather than the minimum six-month period specified in the EBRD and other regional development bank charters. The counterpart provisions of the IBRD, IFC and IDA Articles state that withdrawal takes effect upon receipt by the institution concerned of a withdrawal notice and do not provide for a waiting period between service of the notification and effectiveness of the withdrawal.

In common with the Articles of the other MDBs, the EBRD Agreement provides, in its Article 38, that if a member "fails to fulfil any of its obligations to the Bank," the institution may suspend it from membership; a member so suspended will automatically cease to be a member one year from the date of its suspension unless the Governors decide to restore the member to good standing. Suspension of membership should not be confused with suspension of a member's access to the bank's resources dealt with in Article 8, Paragraph 3 of the Agreement and elaborated on in Chapter Two.[6]

6. *See* pp. 44-45 *supra.*

II. ORGANIZATIONAL STRUCTURE

As the other development banks, the EBRD has a three-tier governing structure, consisting of a Board of Governors, a Board of Directors, and "a President, one or more Vice-Presidents and such other officers and staff as may be considered necessary" (Article 22).

1. Board of Governors

As in the case of the other development banks, the Board of Governors may delegate to the Board of Directors all powers except those reserved to it under the Agreement (Article 24, Paragraph 2). The list of reserved powers in the EBRD is generally similar to that of the ADB and IDB, and is slightly longer than that in the IBRD Articles. The powers which are reserved to the Board of Governors in the EBRD but not in the IBRD are: (i) the power to elect the president of the bank and to determine the salary and other terms of his contract; (ii) the power to approve, after reviewing the auditors' report, the general balance sheet and the statement of profit and loss of the bank; and (iii) the power to determine the reserves. In the IBRD, these powers are exercised by the Executive Directors, whose decision regarding reserves is, in practice, subsequently "noted with approval" by the Board of Governors.

As is the case of the regional development banks, the EBRD Agreement also provides that the Board of Governors retains full power to exercise authority over any matter delegated or assigned to the Board of Directors (Article 24, Paragraph 3). This is understood, but not explicitly mentioned, in the Articles of the IBRD and its affiliates.

The Board of Governors holds an annual meeting and such meetings as may be provided by the Board of Governors or the Board of Directors. The Board of Directors will call meetings of the Board of Governors whenever requested by not less than five members or by members holding not less than one quarter of the total voting power. These provisions are similar to those of the IBRD Articles of Agreement.

2. Board of Directors

i. Composition

The provisions on the size and composition of the Board of Directors ("the Board") (Article 26, Paragraph 1) reflect the various groups of countries which negotiated the Agreement. The initial Board is composed of 23 Directors, of whom:

- eleven are to be elected by the Governors representing the member countries of the EEC, the EEC itself and the EIB;
- twelve are to be elected by Governors representing the other members, of whom:
  - four by the Governors representing countries listed in Annex A as Central and Eastern European countries eligible for assistance from the bank;
  - four by the Governors representing countries listed in Annex A as other European Countries; and
  - four by the Governors representing countries listed in Annex A as Non-European countries.

The Board of Governors may increase or decrease the size of the Board, and modify its composition in order to take account of changes in the number of members of the EBRD by an affirmative vote of not less than two-thirds of the Governors representing not less than three-fourths of the total voting power (Article 26, Paragraph 3). In the IBRD, the majority required to increase the size of the Board is 80% of the total voting power.

Directors hold office for three years (Article 26, Paragraph

5), as is the case in the AfDB and IDB. In the IBRD and the ADB, Executive Directors hold office for two years. The longer period of service provided for in the EBRD Agreement represents an improvement, in view of the complex matters such Boards deal with and the time required by Directors to become familiar with these matters.

ii. Powers

Under Article 27 of the EBRD Agreement, the Board of Directors "shall be responsible for the direction of the general operations of the Bank" and exercises the powers delegated to it by the Board of Governors. While this language is similar to the provisions in the Articles of IBRD and its affiliates, Article 27 states in particular that the Board:

- prepares the work of the Board of Governors;
- in conformity with the general directions of the Board of Governors, establishes policies and takes decisions concerning loans, guarantees, investments in equity capital, borrowing by the bank, furnishing technical assistance and other operations of the bank;
- submits the audited accounts for each financial year for approval of the Board of Governors at each annual meeting; and
- approves the budget.

These more detailed provisions are modelled on those relating to the Board of Directors of the ADB. In practice, the Executive Directors of the IBRD exercise the powers listed above (pursuant to the IBRD By-Laws, the audited accounts are submitted to the Board of Governors for "consideration").

iii. Procedure

The quorum requirement for meetings of the Board of Directors is a majority of the Directors, representing not less than two-thirds of the total voting power (Article 28, Paragraph 2). This is the same as in the AfDB and ADB. In the

IDB, the requirement is of "an absolute majority of the total number of directors, including an absolute majority of the directors of regional members, representing not less than two thirds of the total voting power of the member countries." In the IBRD, the requirement is of a majority of the Directors, exercising not less than one half of the total voting power. As in other MDBs, the Board of EBRD is expected to adopt its rules of procedure in its first meeting.

3. The President, Vice-President(s), Officers and Staff

The President is elected by the Board of Governors (Article 30, Paragraph 1). This is also the case in the ADB and the IDB. In the IBRD and its affiliates as well as in the AfDB, the President is elected by the Executive Directors. The majority required to elect the President of the EBRD is a majority of the total number of Governors representing not less than a majority of the total voting power of the members. This is the same as in the ADB. In the IDB it is a majority in the Board of Directors of the total voting power of the members including an absolute majority of the regional members. In the AfDB, it is a majority of the total voting power of the members. In the IBRD and its affiliates, the President of the IBRD, IFC and MIGA is elected by the Executive Directors by a simple majority of the votes cast (the President of the IBRD is *ex officio* President of IDA).

The term of office of the President of EBRD is *four* years, but he ceases to hold office when the Board of Governors so decides by a vote of not less than two thirds of the Governors exercising not less than two thirds of the total voting power of the members (Article 30, Paragraph 2). In the IBRD and the other regional development banks, the term of office of the President is five years, and the majority required for removal is the same majority required for election.

The description of the functions of the President (Article 30, Paragraphs 4, 5 and 6) follows that of the President of the ADB:

- He is the legal representative of the bank. This is stated in the charters of the other regional development banks. It is also understood in the application of, but is not explicitly stated in, the Articles of Agreement of the IBRD and its affiliates.
- He is the chief of the staff of the bank and is responsible for the organization, appointment and dismissal of the officers and staff "in accordance with regulations to be adopted by the Board of Directors." In the IBRD and its affiliates, the President exercises his powers on organization, appointment and dismissal "subject to the general control of the Executive Directors."
- He conducts, under the general direction of the Board of Directors, "the current business of the Bank".

In the IBRD and its affiliates, the President is the chief of the operating staff of the bank and conducts, under the direction of the Executive Directors, the "ordinary business of the Bank."[7] The slight difference in wording does not seem to suggest substantive differences and the vagueness of the definition of the respective roles of the Board and Management does not seem to be reduced by the new wording. Although it might be argued that the use of the term "current", rather than "ordinary" business implies a narrower scope of responsibilities, such argument does not by itself seem to carry much weight.

7. *Compare*, Articles XII(3) and (4) of the IMF Articles of Agreement as amended in April 1976, effective April 1, 1978. Under these provisions the Executive Board of the IMF is "responsible for conducting the business of the Fund", while the Managing Director "conduct[s], under the direction of the Executive Board, the ordinary business of the Fund." For details on the relevant provisions of the Articles of Agreement of the IBRD and their application in practice, *see* the IBRD Legal Department Memorandum, *The Role of the Executive Directors of the Bank under the Bank's Articles of Agreement and in the Bank's Practice* BPC87-2, October 5, 1987.

The provisions concerning the Vice-Presidents generally follow those in the Articles of Agreement of the ADB. The Board of Directors appoints one or more vice presidents on the recommendation of the President. The term of office, authority, and functions of the vice presidents are also determined by the Board of Directors (Article 31, Paragraph 1). The Articles of Agreement of the IBRD contain no provisions concerning vice presidents. In practice, the vice presidents of the IBRD and its affiliates are appointed by the President. Since 1973 a procedure has been followed in the IBRD whereby the Executive Directors are informed by the President of such appointments five working days before they are made and any Director may call for a discussion of the matter.

The President, vice-president(s), officers and staff, as well as the EBRD itself, "shall in their decisions take into account only considerations relevant to the Bank's purpose, functions and operations, as set out in this Agreement. Such considerations shall be weighed impartially in order to achieve and carry out the purpose and functions of the Bank." As explained earlier, the equivalent provisions of the Articles of Agreement of the other development banks (often under the title "Political Activity Prohibited"), require them and their officers not to interfere in the political affairs of any member or to be influenced in their decisions by the political character of the member or members concerned, and furthermore ordain that "only economic considerations shall be relevant to their decisions, and these considerations shall be weighed impartially". In the IBRD, the General Counsel has expressed the opinion that these provisions, for which there is no counterpart in the EBRD Agreement, are applicable to the Executive Directors.[8]

As in the case of other MDBs, the President and all staff

8. *See* Opinion of the Vice President and General Counsel (Shihata), *Prohibition of Political Activities under the IBRD Articles of Agreement and its Relevance to the Work of the Executive Directors* SecM87-1409, December 23, 1987.

owe their duty to the institution only and members of EBRD are required to respect the international character of this duty and to refrain from any attempt to influence management in the discharge of it (Article 32, Paragraph 3). The temptation to ignore this important provision is far from being theoretical and should be guarded against in practice.

The recruitment of EBRD staff is subject to the requirement, familiar in the Articles of the IBRD and its affiliates, of the "paramount importance of efficiency and technical competence" and of paying due regard to recruitment on a wide geographical basis. However, unlike the IBRD and its affiliates, the EBRD text (Article 30, Paragraph 5) restricts such recruitment on a wide geographical basis to recruitment "among members of the Bank."

4. Voting

Although members of the EBRD are defined in Annex A in categories, votes are not allocated to categories as such.[9] The voting power of each EBRD member is equal to the number of shares it holds (Article 29, Paragraph 1). As was mentioned in Chapter One, a member which fails to pay the instalments due on the paid-in shares loses a percentage of voting power equivalent to the percentage which the amount due but not paid bears to the total amount of paid-in shares subscribed by the member. No similar arrangement exists in the IBRD and its affiliates, except that in the case of IFC the resolutions authorizing additional subscriptions by existing members allowed for payment in full or in instalments, provided that only shares paid for in full would be issued to a subscribing member, and if payment had not

9. For the distinction between the "Bretton Woods Institutions' Pattern", followed in the IBRD and the IMF as well as in the IFC, IDA and regional development banks (with some variation in the case of the ADB) and "the voting blocs formula" adopted in the International Fund for Agricultural Development (IFAD) and initially considered for MIGA, *see* Shihata, *MIGA and Foreign Investment* 304-22 (1988).

been fully made in cash on the date of the last instalment, the subscription of the relevant share became void. In contrast to the other MDBs, there are no "membership votes" in the EBRD. Such votes are normally intended to protect the voting power of small shareholders but lose their importance as the subscribed capital increases, unless they are also increased.

As in the case of the other development banks, the rule in the Board of Governors is that all matters are decided by a majority of the votes cast (Article 29, Paragraph 2). Among the exceptions are: admitting new members, increasing the authorized capital, suspending a member's access to the Bank's resources, increasing the size of the Board of Directors, terminating operations and distributing Bank assets to members, all of which require a special majority of not less than two-thirds of the Governors representing not less than three-fourths of the total voting power. A second group of exceptions, requiring a special majority of not less than two-thirds of the Governors, representing not less than two-thirds of the total voting power, comprises decisions to issue shares at other than par, to allocate net income to purposes other than surplus, and to suspend a member. In addition, a special majority of at least three-fourths of the Governors representing at least 85% of the total voting power is required to permit a member (meaning the Soviet Union) to have access to the Bank's resources beyond certain limits.[10] An even higher majority is required for the amendment of the Agreement as will be explained shortly. The election of the President is subject to a special majority of the total number of Governors, representing not less than a majority of the total voting power.

The special majorities required should be read in the context of the distribution of votes in the EBRD. Assuming full subscription, the Western European members (mem-

10. *See* Chapter Two, pp. 70-72 *supra.*

bers of the EEC, the EEC itself and the EIB) are assured 51% of the votes. Since two-thirds, three-quarters or 85% of the total voting power are needed for approval of the more important decisions, such decisions will need the concurrence of several other members. The recipient countries will have 13.45% of the total votes (presumably to be reduced to 12.17% after the unification of Germany).[11] The U.S. would have 10% of the votes, Japan about 8.52%, Canada 3.4%, the other "European countries" 11.37%, Australia and New Zealand 1.1% and the four developing countries in the non-European category 1.15%. When all shares are subscribed as allocated, the U.S. and Japan acting together would thus have a veto power over the decisions which require 85% of the total voting power. It is important to note however that resort to voting is rather uncommon in the MDBs generally where most decisions are reached through consensus.

In the Board of Directors also, the normal rule is that all matters before the Board are to be decided by "a majority of the voting power of the members voting", i.e. by more than 50 percent of the votes cast. Exceptions are made for "general policy decisions in which cases such policy decisions shall be taken by a majority of not less than two thirds of the total voting power of the members voting" (Article 29, Paragraph 3). With reference to this novel Article, the Chairman's Report contains the following comment:

11. The EBRD Agreement is silent on the fate of the shares allocated to the German Democratic Republic after its unification with the Federal Republic of Germany. Under general international law rules of state succession, and following precedents in the IBRD, IFC and IDA, the unified Germany would succeed to such shares, and the votes associated with them. Members of the EBRD may agree on different arrangements, however, with the consent of the unified Germany. It should be noted that the forthcoming unification is envisaged to be based on a number of legal documents including a joint quadripartite agreement or declaration by the U.S, the U.S.S.R. , the U.K. and France, a treaty between the two Germanys, and the Constitution of the Federal Republic of Germany (Article 23).

"Delegates intended that, in the case of differing views on whether or not issues involved 'general policy', decisions would be made by the Board on the basis of advice from the Legal Counsel. In general, decisions on individual operations would not involve such issues, but 'general policy issues' would include, inter alia, the budget; the annual programme of operations; borrowing policy, including borrowing limits; interest rate policy; exchange risk management policy; the drawing down of notes; underwriting policy and the organizational structure of the Bank".

The above provision of Article 29 and the explanation provided in the Chairman's Report may have been inspired by the IBRD's experience in recent years where some of the examples mentioned proved somewhat controversial and were approved by a not too impressive majority. It is also interesting to note that the "organizational structure of the Bank" is mentioned among the "general policy issues" which require a special majority for their approval. In the IBRD, the General Counsel took the position that the "organization of staff" falls within the powers of the President which he exercises within the directives which the Board may issue in this respect.[12] Surprisingly, the Chairman's Report does not mention "staff compensation policy" among the examples of general policy issues. In the practice of other MDBs, this has often been a divisive issue.

As in the ADB, EBRD Directors representing more than one member may cast separately the votes of the members he or she represents (Article 29, Paragraph 3). In the IBRD and its affiliates, as well as in the IDB and the AfDB, elected Directors must cast their votes as a unit.

A novel feature of the provisions on voting is that a Governor who does not participate in voting in an election

12. *See* Opinion of the Vice President and General Counsel (Shihata), *Responsibility for the Bank's Reorganization*, April 16, 1987.

of Directors may later assign his votes to an elected Director, provided that he first obtains the agreement of all the Governors who have elected the Director concerned. The Director concerned then casts these "assigned" votes (Annex B, Section D, and Article 29, Paragraph 3).

III. STATUS, EXEMPTIONS, IMMUNITIES AND PRIVILEGES

The provisions of the EBRD Agreement concerning the purposes of its status, privileges and immunities (Article 44), as well as the provisions dealing with its status (Article 45), its position with regard to judicial process (Article 46), the immunity of its assets from seizure (Article 47), the immunity of its archives (Article 48), the freedom of its assets from restrictions (Article 49) and its privilege with regard to its official communications (Article 50), are generally similar to those in the Articles of Agreement of the IBRD and its affiliates and in the regional development banks.

1. Judicial Process

Article 46 states the EBRD's position with regard to judicial process. According to this Article:

> "Actions may be brought against the Bank only in a court of competent jurisdiction in the territory of a country in which the Bank has an office, has appointed an agent for the purpose of accepting service or notice of process, or has issued or guaranteed securities. No actions shall, however, be brought by members or persons acting for or deriving claims from members. The property and assets of the Bank shall, wheresoever located and by whomoever held, be immune from all forms of seizure, attachment or execution before the delivery of final judgment against the Bank."

The Chairman's Report contains the following statement in respect of this Article:

> "Delegates noted that this Article was almost exactly the same as Section 3 of Article VII of the I.B.R.D.'s Articles of Agreement. They hoped that courts construing it would draw on the jurisprudence that had evolved in connection with the I.B.R.D.'s Articles".

This would appear to be a reference to judicial precedents,[13] in which U.S. courts concluded that they did not have jurisdiction over the IBRD in suits arising out of its employment relationship with its staff. The same principle is explicitly embodied in Article 44 of the MIGA Convention, which grants MIGA immunity from suits before local courts in respect of personnel matters.

As in the case of the other MDBs, Governors, Directors, Alternates, officers and employees of the EBRD are immune from legal process with respect to acts performed by them in their official capacity (Article 51). As in the case of the AfDB and the ADB, this immunity is specifically extended to experts performing missions for the EBRD (in the IBRD's practice, consultants, i.e. persons appointed for a specified period to carry specific assignments or to satisfy work program needs of limited duration, are given staff appointments and are thus considered as benefitting from the immunities of regular staff).

However, the EBRD Agreement explicitly excludes the immunity with respect to civil liability in the case of damage arising from a road traffic accident caused by any of the persons covered by the general immunity. Such an exclusion is found in a number of other conventions.[14] In the case of the IBRD and its affiliates where no such exclusion

13. Mendaro v. IBRD 717 F.2d 610 (C.A.D.C.,1983); Chiriboga v. IBRD, 616 F. Supp. 963 (D.C.D.C, 1985).

14. *See* e.g., Vienna Convention on Consular Relations, 596 U.N.T.S. 261, April 24, 1963, at Article 43(2).

exists, the immunity is likely to apply only in a few cases as it is enjoyed only when the accident occurs while the staff member is driving in an official capacity. Also, the institution may waive the immunity if the circumstances justify such a waiver. Immunity from legal process is also understood in the case of the staff of the IBRD and its affiliates to cover judicial process as well as quasi judicial orders to attend hearings, such as congressional subpoenas.

2. Privileges of Officers and Employees

As in the other development banks, Article 52 provides the usual privileges to Governors, Directors, Alternates, officers and employees and experts performing missions for the bank, with respect to immigration restrictions, alien registration requirements and national service obligations as well as exchange regulations (Paragraph 1 (i)), and with respect to travel facilities (Paragraph 1 (ii)). However, Paragraph 2 of the same Article also requires the country in which the principal office of the EBRD is located (i.e. the UK) to give the spouse and immediate dependents of these persons who are resident in that country, "opportunity to take employment in that country." In the case of countries in which the bank has an agency or branch office, a similar opportunity is to be made available, "in accordance with the national law of that country." The EBRD is required to negotiate specific agreements implementing these progressive provisions which have no counterpart in the charters of other MDBs.

3. Exemptions from Taxation

i. Exemption of the Bank

As is the case of a number of European conventions (for example the Protocol on the Privileges and Immunities of the European Communities), the provisions of the EBRD regarding its tax immunity are based on a distinction between direct and indirect taxes. By contrast, the charters of the other regional development banks, which are based on the Articles of Agreement of the IBRD, exempt the banks, their assets, income and operations and transactions from all taxation.

Article 53, Paragraph 1 states that within the scope of its official activities, the EBRD, its assets, property and income shall be exempt from all direct taxes. Paragraph 2 provides for an exemption from indirect taxes in the cases in which "purchases or services of substantial value and necessary for the exercise of the official activities of the Bank are made or used by the Bank." To the extent such taxes or duties are identifiable, the member country which has levied them is required to "take appropriate measures to grant exemption from such taxes or duties or to provide for their reimbursement."

Similarly, the EBRD is exempted from all import and export duties and taxes as well as from import and export prohibitions and restrictions with respect to goods "necessary for the exercise of its official activities" (Article 53, Paragraph 3). Also, the EBRD Agreement, like the charters of some other MDBs, provide that the exemptions do not apply to taxes or duties which are no more than charges for public utility services (Article 53, Paragraph 5).

The limitation of the EBRD's tax exemption to activities, goods and services falling within the scope of its "official activities", or required for the exercise of such activities apparently rests on a distinction made in certain European conventions between official and other activities of international organizations for tax exemption purposes. With respect to this Article, the Chairman's Report states as follows:

> "With respect to Article 53, Paragraphs 1, 2 and 3, Delegates shared the view that members would accord the greatest deference to the Bank on whether a Bank activity was 'official' or whether a purchase of goods and services was

'necessary' for the 'official' activities of the Bank; e.g. a duly authorized purchase of goods is to be presumed as 'necessary' for the 'official' activities of the Bank. Beyond this, Delegates shared the view that paragraph 2 was to be interpreted in the light of national practices applicable to international organizations with similar provisions."

The Articles of Agreement of the other MDBs do not make any distinction between official and other activities of the organizations for tax purposes. Indeed such a distinction may be unrealistic. As corporate juridical persons, the activities of international organizations must fall within their purposes and functions and are not otherwise authorized. Barring situations where the organization acts *ultra vires*, which should not be assumed, ancillary activities such as social receptions for staff or visiting delegations are normally considered within the scope of official activities.

ii. Directors, Alternates, Officials and Employees

Article 53, Paragraph 6 establishes a system of "internal taxation" of salaries and emoluments of Directors, Alternates, officials and employees of the EBRD, for the benefit of the institution, and provides that from the date the tax is applied, such salaries and emoluments are exempt from national income tax. Such a system of "internal taxation" is commonly used in European organizations, including the EEC, but is completely unknown in other MDBs.[15] The EBRD Agreement makes a further point in the same Paragraph which is unrelated to the bank itself. It states that "the members may, however, take into account the salaries and emoluments exempted when assessing the amount of tax to be applied to income from other sources." As EBRD will be competing with other MDBs for highly skilled staff, these

15 The U.N. has a system of "staff assessments" which, however, differs from the above described system of "*internal taxation* " in that the beneficiaries of the U.N. assessments are the members states, not the U.N. itself (most of the amounts assessed are used to offset the yearly contribution of member states to the U.N.).

provisions may lead in fact to an unintended result. A higher salary structure in EBRD (to make up for the "internal taxes" or additional national taxation) could hardly have been the objective of the drafters of these provisions.

However, Paragraph 7 of Article 53 allows any member to declare, at the time it deposits its instrument of ratification, acceptance or approval, that it "retains for itself, its political subdivisions or its local authorities the right to tax salaries and emoluments paid by the Bank to citizens or nationals of such member." This provision is similar to the final clause of Article 56(2) ADB. The same Paragraph adds that the Bank is exempt from any obligation for the payment, withholding or collection of such taxes and that it "shall not make any reimbursement for such taxes."

Perhaps as a reflection of recent discussions related to the scope of application of the U.S. estate tax and whether they cover post death pension payments by the IBRD and other international organizations, Article 53, Paragraph 8 specifies that the tax immunity granted on salaries and emoluments does not apply to pensions and annuities paid by the bank. This provision may thus be meant to clarify an ambiguity in the identical exemptions provisions of the charters of other organizations. It should not by itself, however, have a bearing on the interpretation of the relevant provisions in the Articles of the IBRD and its affiliates.[16]

On the subject of taxes on salaries and emoluments, the Chairman's Report states:

> "Delegates took note of the importance placed by some members on their right to tax income derived by their residents who are officers or employees of the Bank. The provisions of paragraphs 6 and 7 of Article 53 do not

16. *See* Memorandum of the (IBRD) Vice President and General Counsel (Shihata), *The Scope of Tax Exemption of 'Salaries and Emoluments' under Section 9(b) of Article VII of the Articles of Agreement of the Bank*, SecM90-53, January 11, 1990.

preclude these members from lodging appropriate reservations in accordance with international law." [17]

iii. Securities

The EBRD Agreement contains provisions exempting securities issued or guaranteed by the bank from certain taxes which are similar to those in the Articles of Agreement of the IBRD and its affiliates and of the other regional development banks. These include taxes which discriminate against the bank's securities solely because they are issued by the bank as well as taxes the jurisdictional basis of which is solely the place or currency in which they are issued, made payable or paid or the location of the office or place of business maintained by the bank (Article 53, Paragraph 9).

iv. Waiver of Immunities, Exemptions and Privileges

Article 55 states that the immunities, privileges and exemptions conferred by the Articles are granted in the interest of the bank, and provides that the Board of Directors may waive any of them in cases in which, in its opinion, this would be in the best interest of the bank. In addition, the President "shall have the right and the duty" to waive any of them in respect of any officer, employee or expert "where, in his or her opinion, the immunity, privilege or exemption would impede the course of justice and can be waived without prejudice to the interests of the Bank."[18]

There is no equivalent provision in the Articles of Agreement of the IBRD, IDA and the IDB but the IFC and MIGA charters authorize such waivers. In the IFC's case, a waiver is authorized in circumstances left to be determined by the Corporation (IFC Article VI(11)), and in MIGA's case in

17. It should be noted that the use of the term "residents" in this context, rather than "nationals" or "citizens", is not in conformity with the provisions of the quoted Article of the EBRD Agreement.

18. It may be noted that the EBRD Agreement is the first among the charters of MDBs, and perhaps among those of international organizations generally, which uses the words "he or she" and "his or her".

circumstances determined by the Agency, where the waiver would not prejudice its interests and, with respect to staff immunities, where the immunity would impede the course of justice. Provisions permitting or requiring waiver of privileges and immunities in specific circumstances are fairly common, and are to be found, for example, in the Articles of Agreement of the AfDB, the ADB and in the Convention on the Privileges and Immunities of the U.N. Specialized Agencies. It is in any event understood in the World Bank Group that privileges and immunities are provided for the benefit of each institution and that the institution maintains an implied power to waive them even when they are stated as privileges for the individuals concerned.

IV. INTERPRETATION; AMENDMENT AND ARBITRATION

1. Interpretation of the Agreement

Article 57 of the EBRD Agreement, like the Articles of other MDBs, provides an internal procedure for the resolution of questions of interpretation or application of the provisions of the Articles that may arise between a member and the bank or between members. Under Article 57, such questions are to be referred in the first instance to the Board of Directors. Any member which is particularly affected by the question under consideration is entitled to direct, non-voting representation at the pertinent Board meeting if the Directors do not include a national of the member concerned. The Directors' decision on such a question of interpretation or application of the Articles may be appealed to the Board of Governors, whose decision on the matter will be final. Pending any such decision by the Governors, the bank may, to the extent it deems necessary, act on the basis of the Directors' decision. These arrangements are similar to the ones in the charters of the other development banks. In practice, there has been no appeal against an interpretations issued by a Board of Directors and such formal interpretations are few indeed.[19]

2. Amendment of the Agreement

Article 56, Paragraph 1 establishes a two-step amendment procedure similar to that in the IBRD and the AfDB, under which amendments are decided by the Board of Governors by the normal voting majority, and then submitted to the members themselves for acceptance. In the EBRD, after amendments have been approved by the Board of Governors, the normal rule is that they must be accepted by not less than three-fourths of the members (including at least two Central or Eastern European members) having not less than four-fifths of the total voting power of the members.[20] In the IBRD, the amendment must, after its approval by the Board of Governors by a simple majority, be accepted by three-fifths of the members exercising 85% of the total voting power. In the AfDB, the majority normally required is two-thirds of the members having three-quarters of the total voting power.

The Articles of Agreement of the ADB, IDB and IFC, and the MIGA Convention, provide a simpler procedure for amendments, which are conditioned only on action of the Board of Governors (the Council of Governors in the case of MIGA). In IFC and in MIGA, the majority required is in

19. In the IBRD practice, following a somewhat active beginning where the Executive Directors established a Committee on Interpretation and issued 13 interpretations in 5 years, only two formal interpretations have been issued since (in 1966 and 1986) and the Board Committee on Interpretation was discontinued.

20. Given that the shares available for subscription by the U.S. represent only 10% of total authorized capital, and assuming full subscription by all potential members, the U.S. will not have in the EBRD the "veto power" in the amendment process which it has enjoyed in the IBRD.

most cases three-fifths of the Governors exercising four-fifths of the total voting power. In the ADB, the normal majority required is two-thirds of the Governors representing not less than three-fourths of the total voting power.

The charters of all these organizations provide exceptions to the normal majority rules described above, in which cases the unanimous consent of the members or the governors, as the case may be, is required. Among the provisions commonly requiring unanimous consent are those on the right to withdraw, the limitation of liability of members and preemptive rights. To this list, the EBRD Agreement adds the purpose and functions of the bank defined in Articles 1 and 2. This addition emphasizes the importance attached by the members to the purpose and functions as presently stated, including the market economy orientation of the institution, elaborated on in Chapter Two.

3. Arbitration

As mentioned above, the EBRD Agreement, like the Articles of the other development banks, provides for the resolution by organs of the bank of questions of interpretation or application of the Articles that may arise between members or between the Bank and a member. The situation is different in respect of disagreements that may arise between the bank and a former member (which would have lost its representation on the organization's Boards) and between the EBRD and members after it has been decided to terminate the bank's operations. As in the case of the Articles of the other MDBs, such disagreements are (under Article 58 of the EBRD Agreement) to be referred to an ad hoc arbitral tribunal consisting of one arbitrator appointed by each party and a third, presiding, arbitrator appointed by a neutral appointing authority. As under the IBRD Articles, this authority is defined in the EBRD Agreement to be the President of the International Court of Justice.[21]

Like the Articles of the other MDBs, the EBRD Agreement contains no special provision on the settlement of disputes that may arise between the bank and recipients of its loans, guarantees and investments.[22] It may, however, be expected that the EBRD, like most other MDBs, will include in its loan, guarantee and investment agreements provisions providing for the resolution of such disputes through negotiation and, failing this (which has not happened in practice), through ad hoc arbitration. In view of the expected prevalence of private sector financing in the EBRD's activities, it may find it unavoidable to submit disputes with private cofinanciers in certain cases to local courts, as the IFC's experience suggests.

21. It may be noted that Article 58 of the EBRD Agreement, like its counterparts in the Articles of the IBRD, IFC, IDA, ADB, AfDB and IDB, does not also empower the designated appointing authority to appoint an arbitrator for a party that fails to do so (the appointing authority appoints only the "third" arbitrator). That this may enable a party to prevent the establishment of the tribunal and thus frustrate the arbitration is illustrated by the advisory opinion rendered in July 1950 by the International Court of Justice in the Case Concerning the Interpretation of Peace Treaties with Bulgaria, Hungary and Romania, 1950 ICJ Rep. 221, which involved arbitration clauses drafted in terms similar to those of Article 58 of the EBRD Agreement and its counterparts in the Articles of the other above-mentioned institutions. The counterpart provisions of the charters of MIGA (Annex II, Article 4) and of the Caribbean Development Bank (Article 60) avoid this risk by also authorizing the appointing authority to appoint an arbitrator for a party declining to do so.

22. *Compare* the MIGA Convention which contains elaborate provisions on the settlement of disputes arising out of the Agency's guarantee operations (Articles 57, 58 and Annex II of the Convention).

Concluding Remarks

The Agreement Establishing the European Bank for Reconstruction and Development is a lengthier and more sophisticated document than the charters of other international financial institutions. It was negotiated, however, in no more than seven days of plenary meetings held within the span of a few months, thus proving once again that positive international action depends first and foremost on the collective political will of participating states.

The EBRD Agreement has led to the creation of the first MDB which would have both the U.S. and the U.S.S.R. as actual members (with 10% and 6% respectively, of the shares and votes).[1] This is also the first international financial institution (other than those whose membership is limited to the European continent) which gives absolute majority, by which most decisions can be taken, to Western European members and ensures that it remains in their hands. Furthermore, it will be the first MDB to limit its assistance to a small number of countries (initially eight, presumably to be reduced to seven after the unification of Germany and, possibly, to six after the first three years of operation to which the USSR access to EBRD resources is limited, unless otherwise decided later on by a special majority). And it will be the first multilateral development bank to condition explicitly its assistance on the application of specified political principles and to provide for certain environmental conditions in its Articles of Agreement.

Such apparent differences from the charters of existing MDBs may not, however, lead the EBRD to operate in a very

1. The U.S.S.R. was among the 45 countries listed in Schedule A of the IBRD Articles of Agreement. It has not, however, subscribed to the shares allocated to it in this Schedule and has not yet joined the IBRD.

different manner from theirs. Nor should they suggest that the EBRD would find it difficult to work closely with the World Bank Group. The IBRD and its affiliates, very much like the EBRD, are cooperative financial institutions where a large portion of capital, and votes, belong to the same group of free market-oriented countries. Support of private sector development and concern for the environment have also been strongly reiterated in recent years as primary concerns for the World Bank Group. Opportunities for joint action between these institutions and the EBRD are therefore expected to override difficulties which may result from the more political features of the EBRD's mandate.

The EBRD Agreement includes important compromises. There is first the significant compromise between those who wanted to limit its operations to the private sector and those who argued for greater flexibility in view of the very limited scope of private enterprises in the recipient countries at present. The agreed text succeeded in preserving the private sector orientation but allowed for financing the public sector within certain quantitative and qualitative limits. Another important compromise is expressed in the provision which allows access to EBRD resources for a limited period of time and for limited purposes to what is described as "any potential recipient country" which requests such limited assistance, but is meant to apply to the USSR only. A third compromise preserved the European character of the institution, both in name, capital *numéraire* and control over most decisions, but ensured that the concurrence of other members holding at least 15.7% of the total votes will be needed to obtain the two-thirds majority required for the "general policy decisions" in the Board of Directors, that the more important decisions of the Board of Governors will be passed by a special majority which requires approval of two-thirds, 75% or 85% of the total votes, and that the U.S. and Japan which together hold 18.5% of the total votes, will, if they act in concert, have a de facto veto power over the fundamental decisions requiring a majority of 85% of the total votes. These and other compromises expressed in the EBRD Agreement seem to have been reached to accommodate different views among the *Western* potential members.

In all, the EBRD Agreement provides a framework which should enable the institution to achieve its purpose and paves the way for an era of greater cooperation among nations whose relationships were until recently characterized by confrontation and animosity. This Agreement is a welcome dividend of the post confrontation era which will hopefully prevail in the 1990s and beyond.

APPENDICES

The EBRD Basic Documents

Appendix I

Agreement Establishing The European Bank for Reconstruction and Development

The Contracting Parties,

Committed to the fundamental principles of multiparty democracy, the rule of law, respect for human rights and market economics;

Recalling the Final Act of the Helsinki Conference on Security and Cooperation in Europe, and in particular its Declaration on Principles;

Welcoming the intent of Central and Eastern European countries to further the practical implementation of multiparty democracy, strengthening democratic institutions, the rule of law and respect for human rights and their willingness to implement reforms in order to evolve towards market-oriented economies;

Considering the importance of close and coordinated cooperation in order to promote the economic progress of Central and Eastern European countries to help their economies become more internationally competitive and assist them in their reconstruction and development and thus to reduce, where appropriate, any risks related to the financing of their economies;

Convinced that the establishment of a multilateral financial institution which is European in its basic character and broadly international in its membership would help serve these ends and would constitute a new and unique structure of cooperation in Europe;

Have agreed to establish hereby the European Bank for Reconstruction and Development (hereinafter called "the Bank") which shall operate in accordance with the following:

Chapter I

PURPOSE, FUNCTIONS AND MEMBERSHIP

Article 1

PURPOSE

In contributing to economic progress and reconstruction, the purpose of the Bank shall be to foster the transition towards open market-oriented economies and to promote private and entrepreneurial initiative in the Central and Eastern European countries committed to and applying the principles of multiparty democracy, pluralism and market economics.

Article 2

FUNCTIONS

1. To fulfil on a long-term basis its purpose of fostering the transition of Central and Eastern European countries towards open market-oriented economies and the promotion of private and entrepreneurial initiative, the Bank shall assist the recipient member countries to implement structural and sectoral economic reforms, including demonopolization, decentralization and privatization, to help their economies become fully integrated into the international economy by measures:

(i) to promote, through private and other interested investors, the establishment, improvement and expansion of productive, competitive and private sector activity, in particular small and medium sized enterprises;

(ii) to mobilize domestic and foreign capital and experienced management to the end described in (i);

(iii) to foster productive investment, including in the service and financial sectors, and in related infrastructure where that is necessary to support private and entrepreneurial initiative, thereby assisting in making a competitive environment and raising productivity, the standard of living and conditions of labour;
(iv) to provide technical assistance for the preparation, financing and implementation of relevant projects, whether individual or in the context of specific investment programmes;
(v) to stimulate and encourage the development of capital markets;
(vi) to give support to sound and economically viable projects involving more than one recipient member country;
(vii) to promote in the full range of its activities environmentally sound and sustainable development; and
(viii) to undertake such other activities and provide such other services as may further these functions.

2. In carrying out the functions referred to in paragraph 1 of this Article, the Bank shall work in close cooperation with all its members and, in such manner as it may deem appropriate within the terms of this Agreement, with the International Monetary Fund, the International Bank for Reconstruction and Development, the International Finance Corporation, the Multilateral Investment Guarantee Agency, and the Organization for Economic Cooperation and Development, and shall cooperate with the United Nations and its Specialised Agencies and other related bodies, and any entity, whether public or private, concerned with the economic development of, and investment in, Central and Eastern European countries.

Article 3

MEMBERSHIP

1. Membership in the Bank shall be open:

(i) to (1) European countries and (2) non-European countries which are members of the International Monetary Fund; and
(ii) to the European Economic Community and the European Investment Bank.

2. Countries eligible for membership under paragraph 1 of this Article, which do not become members in accordance with Article 61 of this Agreement, may be admitted, under such terms and conditions as the Bank may determine, to membership in the Bank upon the affirmative vote of not less than two-thirds of the Governors, representing not less than three-fourths of the total voting power of the members.

Chapter II

CAPITAL

Article 4

AUTHORIZED CAPITAL STOCK

1. The original authorized capital stock shall be ten thousand million (10,000,000,000) ECU. It shall be divided into one million (1,000,000) shares, having a par value of ten thousand (10,000) ECU each, which shall be available for subscription only by members in accordance with the provisions of Article 5 of this Agreement.

2. The original capital stock shall be divided into paid-in shares and callable shares. The initial total aggregate par value of paid-in shares shall be three thousand million (3,000,000,000) ECU.

3. The authorized capital stock may be increased at such time and under such terms as may seem advisable, by a vote of not less

than two-thirds of the Governors, representing not less than three-fourths of the total voting power of the members.

Article 5

SUBSCRIPTION OF SHARES

1. Each member shall subscribe to shares of the capital stock of the Bank, subject to fulfilment of the member's legal requirements. Each subscription to the original authorized capital stock shall be for paid-in shares and callable shares in the proportion of three (3) to seven (7). The initial number of shares available to be subscribed to by Signatories to this Agreement which become members in accordance with Article 61 of this Agreement shall be that set forth in Annex A. No member shall have an initial subscription of less than one hundred (100) shares.

2. The initial number of shares to be subscribed to by countries which are admitted to membership in accordance with paragraph 2 of Article 3 of this Agreement shall be determined by the Board of Governors; provided, however, that no such subscription shall be authorized which would have the effect of reducing the percentage of capital stock held by countries which are members of the European Economic Community, together with the European Economic Community and the European Investment Bank, below the majority of the total subscribed capital stock.

3. The Board of Governors shall at intervals of not more than five (5) years review the capital stock of the Bank. In case of an increase in the authorized capital stock, each member shall have a reasonable opportunity to subscribe, under such uniform terms and conditions as the Board of Governors shall determine, to a proportion of the increase in stock equivalent to the proportion which its stock subscribed bears to the total subscribed capital stock immediately prior to such increase. No member shall be obliged to subscribe to any part of an increase of capital stock.

4. Subject to the provisions of paragraph 3 of this Article, the Board of Governors may, at the request of a member, increase the subscription of that member, or allocate shares to that member within the authorized capital stock which are not taken up by other members; provided, however, that such increase shall not

have the effect of reducing the percentage of capital stock held by countries which are members of the European Economic Community, together with the European Economic Community and the European Investment Bank, below the majority of the total subscribed capital stock.

5. Shares of stock initially subscribed to by members shall be issued at par. Other shares shall be issued at par unless the Board of Governors, by a vote of not less than two-thirds of the Governors, representing not less than two-thirds of the total voting power of the members, decides to issue them in special circumstances on other terms.

6. Shares of stock shall not be pledged or encumbered in any manner whatsoever, and they shall not be transferable except to the Bank in accordance with Chapter VII of this Agreement.

7. The liability of the members on shares shall be limited to the unpaid portion of their issue price. No member shall be liable, by reason of its membership, for obligations of the Bank.

Article 6

PAYMENT OF SUBSCRIPTIONS

1. Payment of the paid-in shares of the amount initially subscribed to by each Signatory to this Agreement, which becomes a member in accordance with Article 61 of this Agreement, shall be made in five (5) instalments of twenty (20) per cent each of such amount. The first instalment shall be paid by each member within sixty (60) days after the date of the entry into force of this Agreement, or after the date of deposit of its instrument of ratification, acceptance or approval in accordance with Article 61, if this latter is later than the date of the entry into force. The remaining four (4) instalments shall each become due successively one year from the date on which the preceding instalment became due and shall each, subject to the legislative requirements of each member, be paid.

2. Fifty (50) per cent of payment of each instalment pursuant to paragraph 1 of this Article, or by a member admitted in accordance with paragraph 2 of Article 3 of this Agreement, may be made in promissory notes or other obligations issued by such member and denominated in ECU, in United States dollars or in

Japanese yen, to be drawn down as the Bank needs funds for disbursement as a result of its operations. Such notes or obligations shall be non-negotiable, non-interest-bearing and payable to the Bank at par value upon demand. Demands upon such notes or obligations shall, over reasonable periods of time, be made so that the value of such demands in ECU at the time of demand from each member is proportional to the number of paid-in shares subscribed to and held by each such member depositing such notes or obligations.

3. All payment obligations of a member in respect of subscription to shares in the initial capital stock shall be settled either in ECU, in United States dollars or in Japanese yen on the basis of the average exchange rate of the relevant currency in terms of the ECU for the period from 30 September 1989 to 31 March 1990 inclusive.

4. Payment of the amount subscribed to the callable capital stock of the Bank shall be subject to call, taking account of Articles 17 and 42 of this Agreement, only as and when required by the Bank to meet its liabilities.

5. In the event of a call referred to in paragraph 4 of this Article, payment shall be made by the member in ECU, in United States dollars or in Japanese yen. Such calls shall be uniform in ECU value upon each callable share calculated at the time of the call.

6. The Bank shall determine the place for any payment under this Article not later than one month after the inaugural meeting of its Board of Governors, provided that, before such determination, the payment of the first instalment referred to in paragraph 1 of this Article shall be made to the European Investment Bank, as trustee for the Bank.

7. For subscriptions other than those described in paragraphs 1, 2 and 3 of this Article, payments by a member in respect of subscription to paid-in shares in the authorized capital stock shall be made in ECU, in United States dollars or in Japanese yen whether in cash or in promissory notes or in other obligations.

8. For the purposes of this Article, payment or denomination in ECU shall include payment or denomination in any fully convertible currency which is equivalent on the date of payment or encashment to the value of the relevant obligation in ECU.

Article 7

ORDINARY CAPITAL RESOURCES

As used in this Agreement, the term "ordinary capital resources" of the Bank shall include the following:

(i) authorized capital stock of the Bank, including both paid-in and callable shares, subscribed to pursuant to Article 5 of this Agreement;

(ii) funds raised by borrowings of the Bank by virtue of powers conferred by sub-paragraph (i) of Article 20 of this Agreement, to which the commitment to calls provided for in paragraph 4 of Article 6 of this Agreement is applicable;

(iii) funds received in repayment of loans or guarantees and proceeds from the disposal of equity investment made with the resources indicated in sub-paragraphs (i) and (ii) of this Article;

(iv) income derived from loans and equity investment, made from the resources indicated in sub-paragraphs (i) and (ii) of this Article, and income derived from guarantees and underwriting not forming part of the special operations of the Bank; and

(v) any other funds or income received by the Bank which do not form part of its Special Funds resources referred to in Article 19 of this Agreement.

Chapter III

OPERATIONS

Article 8

RECIPIENT COUNTRIES AND USE OF RESOURCES

1. The resources and facilities of the Bank shall be used exclusively to implement the purpose and carry out the functions set forth, respectively, in Articles 1 and 2 of this Agreement.

2. The Bank may conduct its operations in countries from Central and Eastern Europe which are proceeding steadily in the transition towards market-oriented economies and the promotion of private and entrepreneurial initiative, and which apply, by concrete steps and otherwise, the principles as set forth in Article 1 of this Agreement.

3. In cases where a member might be implementing policies which are inconsistent with Article 1 of this Agreement, or in exceptional circumstances, the Board of Directors shall consider whether access by a member to Bank resources should be suspended or otherwise modified and may make recommendations accordingly to the Board of Governors. Any decision on these matters shall be taken by the Board of Governors by a majority of not less than two-thirds of the Governors, representing not less than three-fourths of the total voting power of the members.

4. (i) Any potential recipient country may request that the Bank provide access to its resources for limited purposes over a period of three (3) years beginning after the entry into force of this Agreement. Any such request shall be attached as an integral part of this Agreement as soon as it is made.

(ii) During such a period:

(a) the Bank shall provide to such a country, and to enterprises in its territory, upon their request, technical assistance and other types of assistance directed to finance its private sector, to facilitate the transition of state-owned enterprises to private ownership and control, and to help enterprises operating competitively and moving to participation in the market oriented economy, subject to the proportion set forth in paragraph 3 of Article 11 of this Agreement;

(b) the total amount of any assistance thus provided shall not exceed the total amount of cash disbursed and promissory notes issued by that country for its shares.

(iii) At the end of this period, the decision to allow such a country access beyond the limits specified in subparagraphs (a) and (b) shall be taken by the Board of Governors by a majority of not less than three-fourths of the Governors representing not less than eighty-five (85) per cent of the total voting power of the members.

Article 9

ORDINARY AND SPECIAL OPERATIONS

The operations of the Bank shall consist of ordinary operations financed from the ordinary capital resources of the Bank referred to in Article 7 of this Agreement and special operations financed from the Special Funds resources referred to in Article 19 of this Agreement. The two types of operations may be combined.

Article 10

SEPARATION OF OPERATIONS

1. The ordinary capital resources and the Special Funds resources of the Bank shall at all times and in all respects be held, used, committed, invested or otherwise disposed of entirely separately from each other. The financial statements of the Bank shall show the reserves of the Bank, together with its ordinary operations, and, separately, its special operations.

2. The ordinary capital resources of the Bank shall under no circumstances be charged with, or used to discharge, losses or liabilities arising out of special operations or other activities for which Special Funds resources were originally used or committed.

3. Expenses appertaining directly to ordinary operations shall be charged to the ordinary capital resources of the Bank. Expenses appertaining directly to special operations shall be charged to Special Funds resources. Any other expenses shall, subject to paragraph 1 of Article 18 of this Agreement, be charged as the Bank shall determine.

Article 11

METHODS OF OPERATION

1. The Bank shall carry out its operations in furtherance of its purpose and functions as set out in Articles 1 and 2 of this Agreement in any or all of the following ways:

(i) by making, or cofinancing together with multilateral institutions, commercial banks or other interested sources, or participating in, loans to private sector enterprises, loans to any state-owned enterprise operating competitively and moving to participation in the market-oriented economy, and loans to any state-owned enterprise to facilitate its transition to private ownership and control; in particular to facilitate or enhance the participation of private and/or foreign capital in such enterprises;

(ii) (a) by investment in the equity capital of private sector enterprises;

(b) by investment in the equity capital of any state-owned enterprise operating competitively and moving to participation in the market-oriented economy, and investment in the equity capital of any state-owned enterprise to facilitate its transition to private ownership and control; in particular to facilitate or enhance the participation of private and/or foreign capital in such enterprises; and

(c) by underwriting, where other means of financing are not appropriate, the equity issue of securities by both private sector enterprises and such state-owned enterprises referred to in (b) above for the ends mentioned in that sub-paragraph;

(iii) by facilitating access to domestic and international capital markets by private sector enterprises or by other enterprises referred to in subparagraph (i) of this paragraph for the ends mentioned in that sub-paragraph, through the provision of guarantees, where other means of financing are not appropriate, and through financial advice and other forms of assistance;

(iv) by deploying Special Funds resources in accordance with the agreements determining their use; and

(v) by making or participating in loans and providing technical assistance for the reconstruction or development of infrastructure, including environmental programmes, necessary for private sector development and the transition to a market-oriented economy.

For the purposes of this paragraph, a state-owned enterprise shall not be regarded as operating competitively unless it operates autonomously in a competitive market environment and unless it is subject to bankruptcy laws.

2. (i) The Board of Directors shall review at least annually the Bank's operations and lending strategy in each recipient country to ensure that the purpose and the functions of the Bank, as set out in Articles 1 and 2 of this Agreement, are fully served. Any decision pursuant to such a review shall be taken by a majority of not less than two-thirds of the Directors, representing not less than three-fourths of the total voting power of the members.

(ii) The said review shall involve the consideration of, *inter alia*, each recipient country's progress made on decentralization, demonopolization and privatization and the relative shares of the Bank's lending to private enterprises, to state-owned enterprises in the process of transition to participation in the market-oriented economy or privatization, for infrastructure, for technical assistance, and for other purposes.

3. (i) Not more than forty (40) per cent of the amount of the Bank's total committed loans, guarantees and equity investments, without prejudice to its other operations referred to in this Article, shall be provided to the state sector. Such percentage limit shall apply initially over a two (2) year period, from the date of commencement of the Bank's operations,

taking one year with another, and thereafter in respect of each subsequent financial year.

(ii) For any country, not more than forty (40) per cent of the amount of the Bank's total committed loans, guarantees and equity investments over a period of five (5) years, taking one year with another, and without prejudice to the Bank's other operations referred to in this Article, shall be provided to the state sector.

(iii) For the purposes of this paragraph,

(a) the state sector includes national and local governments, their agencies, and enterprises owned or controlled by any of them;

(b) a loan or guarantee to, or equity investment in, a state-owned enterprise which is implementing a programme to achieve private ownership and control shall not be considered as made to the state sector;

(c) loans to a financial intermediary for onlending to the private sector shall not be considered as made to the state sector.

Article 12

LIMITATIONS ON ORDINARY OPERATIONS

1. The total amount of outstanding loans, equity investments and guarantees made by the Bank in its ordinary operations shall not be increased at any time, if by such increase the total amount of its unimpaired subscribed capital, reserves and surpluses included in its ordinary capital resources would be exceeded.

2. The amount of any equity investment shall not normally exceed such percentage of the equity capital of the enterprise concerned as shall be determined, by a general rule, to be appropriate by the Board of Directors. The Bank shall not seek to obtain by such an investment a controlling interest in the enterprise concerned and shall not exercise such control or assume direct responsibility for managing any enterprise in which it has an investment, except in the event of actual or threatened default on any of its investments, actual or threatened insolvency

of the enterprise in which such investment shall have been made, or other situations which, in the opinion of the Bank, threaten to jeopardize such investment, in which case the Bank may take such action and exercise such rights as it may deem necessary for the protection of its interests.

3. The amount of the Bank's disbursed equity investments shall not at any time exceed an amount corresponding to its total unimpaired paid-in subscribed capital, surpluses and general reserve.

4. The Bank shall not issue guarantees for export credits nor undertake insurance activities.

Article 13

OPERATING PRINCIPLES

The Bank shall operate in accordance with the following principles:

(i) the Bank shall apply sound banking principles to all its operations;

(ii) the operations of the Bank shall provide for the financing of specific projects, whether individual or in the context of specific investment programmes, and for technical assistance, designed to fulfil its purpose and functions as set out in Articles 1 and 2 of this Agreement;

(iii) the Bank shall not finance any undertaking in the territory of a member if that member objects to such financing;

(iv) the Bank shall not allow a disproportionate amount of its resources to be used for the benefit of any member;

(v) the Bank shall seek to maintain reasonable diversification in all its investments;

(vi) before a loan, guarantee or equity investment is granted, the applicant shall have submitted an adequate proposal and the President of the Bank shall have presented to the Board of Directors a written report regarding the proposal, together with recommendations, on the basis of a staff study;

(vii) the Bank shall not undertake any financing, or provide any facilities, when the applicant is able to obtain sufficient financing or facilities elsewhere on terms and conditions that the Bank considers reasonable;

(viii) in providing or guaranteeing financing, the Bank shall pay due regard to the prospect that the borrower and its guarantor, if any, will be in a position to meet their obligations under the financing contract;

(ix) in case of a direct loan made by the Bank, the borrower shall be permitted by the Bank to draw its funds only to meet expenditure as it is actually incurred;

(x) the Bank shall seek to revolve its funds by selling its investments to private investors whenever it can appropriately do so on satisfactory terms;

(xi) in its investments in individual enterprises, the Bank shall undertake its financing on terms and conditions which it considers appropriate, taking into account the requirements of the enterprise, the risks being undertaken by the Bank, and the terms and conditions normally obtained by private investors for similar financing;

(xii) the Bank shall place no restriction upon the procurement of goods and services from any country from the proceeds of any loan, investment or other financing undertaking in the ordinary or special operations of the Bank, and shall, in all appropriate cases, make its loans and other operations conditional on international invitations to tender being arranged; and

(xiii) the Bank shall take the necessary measures to ensure that the proceeds of any loan made, guaranteed or participated in by the Bank, or any equity investment, are used only for the purposes for which the loan or the equity investment was granted and with due attention to considerations of economy and efficiency.

Article 14

TERMS AND CONDITIONS FOR LOANS AND GUARANTEES

1. In the case of loans made, participated in, or guaranteed by the Bank, the contract shall establish the terms and conditions for the loan or the guarantee concerned, including those relating to payment of principal, interest and other fees, charges, maturities and dates of payment in respect of the loan or the guarantee, respectively. In setting such terms and conditions, the Bank shall take fully into account the need to safeguard its income.

2. Where the recipient of loans or guarantees of loans is not itself a member, but is a state-owned enterprise, the Bank may, when it appears desirable, bearing in mind the different approaches appropriate to public and state-owned enterprises in transition to private ownership and control, require the member or members in whose territory the project concerned is to be carried out, or a public agency or any instrumentality of such member or members acceptable to the Bank, to guarantee the repayment of the principal and the payment of interest and other fees and charges of the loan in accordance with the terms thereof. The Board of Directors shall review annually the Bank's practice in this matter, paying due attention to the Bank's creditworthiness.

3. The loan or guarantee contract shall expressly state the currency or currencies, or ECU, in which all payments to the Bank thereunder shall be made.

Article 15

COMMISSION AND FEES

1. The Bank shall charge, in addition to interest, a commission on loans made or participated in as part of its ordinary operations. The terms and conditions of this commission shall be determined by the Board of Directors.

2. In guaranteeing a loan as part of its ordinary operations, or in underwriting the sale of securities, the Bank shall charge fees, payable at rates and times determined by the Board of Directors, to provide suitable compensation for its risks.

3. The Board of Directors may determine any other charges

of the Bank in its ordinary operations and any commission, fees or other charges in its special operations.

Article 16

SPECIAL RESERVE

1. The amount of commissions and fees received by the Bank pursuant to Article 15 of this Agreement shall be set aside as a special reserve which shall be kept for meeting the losses of the Bank in accordance with Article 17 of this Agreement. The special reserve shall be held in such liquid form as the Bank may decide.

2. If the Board of Directors determines that the size of the special reserve is adequate, it may decide that all or part of the said commission or fees shall henceforth form part of the income of the Bank.

Article 17

METHODS OF MEETING THE LOSSES OF THE BANK

1. In the Bank's ordinary operations, in cases of arrears or default on loans made, participated in, or guaranteed by the Bank, and in cases of losses on underwriting and in equity investment, the Bank shall take such action as it deems appropriate. The Bank shall maintain appropriate provisions against possible losses.

2. Losses arising in the Bank's ordinary operations shall be charged:

(i) first, to the provisions referred to in paragraph 1 of this Article;
(ii) second, to net income;
(iii) third, against the special reserve provided for in Article 16 of this Agreement;
(iv) fourth, against its general reserve and surpluses;
(v) fifth, against the unimpaired paid-in capital; and
(vi) last, against an appropriate amount of the uncalled subscribed callable capital which shall be called in accordance with the provisions of paragraphs 4 and 5 of Article 6 of this Agreement.

Article 18

SPECIAL FUNDS

1. The Bank may accept the administration of Special Funds which are designed to serve the purpose and come within the functions of the Bank. The full cost of administering any such Special Fund shall be charged to that Special Fund.

2. Special Funds accepted by the Bank may be used in any manner and on any terms and conditions consistent with the purpose and the functions of the Bank, with the other applicable provisions of this Agreement, and with the agreement or agreements relating to such Funds.

3. The Bank shall adopt such rules and regulations as may be required for the establishment, administration and use of each Special Fund. Such rules and regulations shall be consistent with the provisions of this Agreement, except for those provisions expressly applicable only to ordinary operations of the Bank.

Article 19

SPECIAL FUNDS RESOURCES

The term "Special Funds resources" shall refer to the resources of any Special Fund and shall include:

(i) funds accepted by the Bank for inclusion in any Special Fund;

(ii) funds repaid in respect of loans or guarantees, and the proceeds of equity investments, financed from the resources of any Special Fund which, under the rules and regulations governing that Special Fund, are received by such Special Fund; and

(iii) income derived from investment of Special Funds resources.

Chapter IV

BORROWING AND OTHER MISCELLANEOUS POWERS

Article 20

GENERAL POWERS

1. The Bank shall have, in addition to the powers specified elsewhere in this Agreement, the power to:

- (i) borrow funds in member countries or elsewhere, provided always that:
  - (a) before making a sale of its obligations in the territory of a country, the Bank shall have obtained its approval; and
  - (b) where the obligations of the Bank are to be denominated in the currency of a member, the Bank shall have obtained its approval;
- (ii) invest or deposit funds not needed in its operations;
- (iii) buy and sell securities, in the secondary market, which the Bank has issued or guaranteed or in which it has invested;
- (iv) guarantee securities in which it has invested in order to facilitate their sale;
- (v) underwrite, or participate in the underwriting of, securities issued by any enterprise for purposes consistent with the purpose and functions of the Bank;
- (vi) provide technical advice and assistance which serve its purpose and come within its functions;
- (vii) exercise such other powers and adopt such rules and regulations as may be necessary or appropriate in furtherance of its purpose and functions, consistent with the provisions of this Agreement; and
- (viii) conclude agreements of cooperation with any public or private entity or entities.

2. Every security issued or guaranteed by the Bank shall bear on its face a conspicuous statement to the effect that it is not an

obligation of any Government or member, unless it is in fact the obligation of a particular Government or member, in which case it shall so state.

Chapter V

CURRENCIES

Article 21

DETERMINATION AND USE OF CURRENCIES

1. Whenever it shall become necessary under this Agreement to determine whether any currency is fully convertible for the purposes of this Agreement, such determination shall be made by the Bank, taking into account the paramount need to preserve its own financial interests, after consultation, if necessary, with the International Monetary Fund.

2. Members shall not impose any restrictions on the receipt, holding, use or transfer by the Bank of the following:

- (i) currencies or ECU received by the Bank in payment of subscriptions to its capital stock, in accordance with Article 6 of this Agreement;
- (ii) currencies obtained by the Bank by borrowing;
- (iii) currencies and other resources administered by the Bank as contributions to Special Funds; and
- (iv) currencies received by the Bank in payment on account of principal, interest, dividends or other charges in respect of loans or investments, or the proceeds of disposal of such investments made out of any of the funds referred to in sub-paragraphs (i) to (iii) of this paragraph, or in payment of commission, fees or other charges.

Chapter VI

ORGANIZATION AND MANAGEMENT

Article 22

STRUCTURE

The Bank shall have a Board of Governors, a Board of Directors, a President, one or more Vice-Presidents and such other officers and staff as may be considered necessary.

Article 23

BOARD OF GOVERNORS: COMPOSITION

1. Each member shall be represented on the Board of Governors and shall appoint one Governor and one Alternate. Each Governor and Alternate shall serve at the pleasure of the appointing member. No Alternate may vote except in the absence of his or her principal. At each of its annual meetings, the Board shall elect one of the Governors as Chairman who shall hold office until the election of the next Chairman.

2. Governors and Alternates shall serve as such without remuneration from the Bank.

Article 24

BOARD OF GOVERNORS: POWERS

1. All the powers of the Bank shall be vested in the Board of Governors.

2. The Board of Governors may delegate to the Board of Directors any or all of its powers, except the power to:

- (i) admit new members and determine the conditions of their admission;
- (ii) increase or decrease the authorized capital stock of the Bank;
- (iii) suspend a member;

(iv) decide appeals from interpretations or applications of this Agreement given by the Board of Directors;
(v) authorize the conclusion of general agreements for co-operation with other international organizations;
(vi) elect the Directors and the President of the Bank;
(vii) determine the remuneration of the Directors and Alternate Directors and the salary and other terms of the contract of service of the President;
(viii) approve, after reviewing the auditors' report, the general balance sheet and the statement of profit and loss of the Bank;
(ix) determine the reserves and the allocation and distribution of the net profits of the Bank;
(x) amend this Agreement;
(xi) decide to terminate the operations of the Bank and to distribute its assets; and
(xii) exercise such other powers as are expressly assigned to the Board of Governors in this Agreement.

3. The Board of Governors shall retain full power to exercise authority over any matter delegated or assigned to the Board of Directors under paragraph 2 of this Article, or elsewhere in this Agreement.

Article 25

BOARD OF GOVERNORS: PROCEDURE

1. The Board of Governors shall hold an annual meeting and such other meetings as may be provided for by the Board or called by the Board of Directors. Meetings of the Board of Governors shall be called, by the Board of Directors, whenever requested by not less than five (5) members of the Bank or members holding not less than one quarter of the total voting power of the members.

2. Two-thirds of the Governors shall constitute a quorum for any meeting of the Board of Governors, provided such majority represents not less than two-thirds of the total voting power of the members.

3. The Board of Governors may by regulation establish a procedure whereby the Board of Directors may, when the latter

deems such action advisable, obtain a vote of the Governors on a specific question without calling a meeting of the Board of Governors.

4. The Board of Governors, and the Board of Directors to the extent authorized, may adopt such rules and regulations and establish such subsidiary bodies as may be necessary or appropriate to conduct the business of the Bank.

Article 26

BOARD OF DIRECTORS: COMPOSITION

1. The Board of Directors shall be composed of twenty-three (23) members who shall not be members of the Board of Governors, and of whom:

- (i) Eleven (11) shall be elected by the Governors representing Belgium, Denmark, France, the Federal Republic of Germany, Greece, Ireland, Italy, Luxembourg, the Netherlands, Portugal, Spain, the United Kingdom, the European Economic Community and the European Investment Bank; and
- (ii) Twelve (12) shall be elected by the Governors representing other members, of whom:
  - (a) four (4), by the Governors representing those countries listed in Annex A as Central and Eastern European countries eligible for assistance from the Bank;
  - (b) four (4), by the Governors representing those countries listed in Annex A as other European countries;
  - (c) four (4), by the Governors representing those countries listed in Annex A as non-European countries.

Directors, as well as representing members whose Governors have elected them, may also represent members who assign their votes to them.

2. Directors shall be persons of high competence in economic and financial matters and shall be elected in accordance with Annex B.

3. The Board of Governors may increase or decrease the size, or revise the composition, of the Board of Directors, in order to take into account changes in the number of members of the Bank, by an affirmative vote of not less than two-thirds of the Governors, representing not less than three-fourths of the total voting power of the members. Without prejudice to the exercise of these powers for subsequent elections, the number and composition of the second Board of Directors shall be as set out in paragraph 1 of this Article.

4. Each Director shall appoint an Alternate with full power to act for him or her when he or she is not present. Directors and Alternates shall be nationals of member countries. No member shall be represented by more than one Director. An Alternate may participate in meetings of the Board but may vote only when he or she is acting in place of his or her principal.

5. Directors shall hold office for a term of three (3) years and may be reelected; provided that the first Board of Directors shall be elected by the Board of Governors at its inaugural meeting, and shall hold office until the next immediately following annual meeting of the Board of Governors or, if that Board shall so decide at that annual meeting, until its next subsequent annual meeting. They shall continue in office until their successors shall have been chosen and assumed office. If the office of a Director becomes vacant more than one hundred and eighty (180) days before the end of his or her term, a successor shall be chosen in accordance with Annex B, for the remainder of the term, by the Governors who elected the former Director. A majority of the votes cast by such Governors shall be required for such election. If the office of a Director becomes vacant one hundred and eighty (180) days or less before the end of his or her term, a successor may similarly be chosen for the remainder of the term, by the votes cast by such Governors who elected the former Director, in which election a majority of the votes cast by such Governors shall be required. While the office remains vacant, the Alternate of the former Director shall exercise the powers of the latter, except that of appointing an Alternate.

Article 27

BOARD OF DIRECTORS: POWERS

Without prejudice to the powers of the Board of Governors as provided in Article 24 of this Agreement, the Board of Directors shall be responsible for the direction of the general operations of the Bank and, for this purpose, shall, in addition to the powers assigned to it expressly by this Agreement, exercise all the powers delegated to it by the Board of Governors, and in particular:

(i) prepare the work of the Board of Governors;
(ii) in conformity with the general directions of the Board of Governors, establish policies and take decisions concerning loans, guarantees, investments in equity capital, borrowing by the Bank, the furnishing of technical assistance, and other operations of the Bank;
(iii) submit the audited accounts for each financial year for approval of the Board of Governors at each annual meeting; and
(iv) approve the budget of the Bank.

Article 28

BOARD OF DIRECTORS: PROCEDURE

1. The Board of Directors shall normally function at the principal office of the Bank and shall meet as often as the business of the Bank may require.

2. A majority of the Directors shall constitute a quorum for any meeting of the Board of Directors, provided such majority represents not less than two-thirds of the total voting power of the members.

3. The Board of Governors shall adopt regulations under which, if there is no Director of its nationality, a member may send a representative to attend, without right to vote, any meeting of the Board of Directors when a matter particularly affecting that member is under consideration.

Article 29

VOTING

1. The voting power of each member shall be equal to the number of its subscribed shares in the capital stock of the Bank. In the event of any member failing to pay any part of the amount due in respect of its obligations in relation to paid-in shares under Article 6 of this Agreement, such member shall be unable for so long as such failure continues to exercise that percentage of its voting power which corresponds to the percentage which the amount due but unpaid bears to the total amount of paid-in shares subscribed to by that member in the capital stock of the Bank.

2. In voting in the Board of Governors, each Governor shall be entitled to cast the votes of the member he or she represents. Except as otherwise expressly provided in this Agreement, all matters before the Board of Governors shall be decided by a majority of the voting power of the members voting.

3. In voting in the Board of Directors each Director shall be entitled to cast the number of votes to which the Governors who have elected him or her are entitled and those to which any Governors who have assigned their votes to him or her, pursuant to Section D of Annex B, are entitled. A Director representing more than one member may cast separately the votes of the members he or she represents. Except as otherwise expressly provided in this Agreement, and except for general policy decisions in which cases such policy decisions shall be taken by a majority of not less than two-thirds of the total voting power of the members voting, all matters before the Board of Directors shall be decided by a majority of the voting power of the members voting.

Article 30

THE PRESIDENT

1. The Board of Governors, by a vote of a majority of the total number of Governors, representing not less than a majority of the total voting power of the members, shall elect a President of the

Bank. The President, while holding office, shall not be a Governor or a Director or an Alternate for either.

2. The term of office of the President shall be four (4) years. He or she may be re-elected. He or she shall, however, cease to hold office when the Board of Governors so decides by an affirmative vote of not less than two-thirds of the Governors, representing not less than two-thirds of the total voting power of the members. If the office of the President for any reason becomes vacant, the Board of Governors, in accordance with the provisions of paragraph 1 of this Article, shall elect a successor for up to four (4) years.

3. The President shall not vote, except that he or she may cast a deciding vote in case of an equal division. He or she may participate in meetings of the Board of Governors and shall chair the meetings of the Board of Directors.

4. The President shall be the legal representative of the Bank.

5. The President shall be chief of the staff of the Bank. He or she shall be responsible for the organization, appointment and dismissal of the officers and staff in accordance with regulations to be adopted by the Board of Directors. In appointing officers and staff, he or she shall, subject to the paramount importance of efficiency and technical competence, pay due regard to recruitment on a wide geographical basis among members of the Bank.

6. The President shall conduct, under the direction of the Board of Directors, the current business of the Bank.

Article 31

VICE PRESIDENT (S)

1. One or more Vice-Presidents shall be appointed by the Board of Directors on the recommendation of the President. A Vice-President shall hold office for such term, exercise such authority and perform such functions in the administration of the Bank, as may be determined by the Board of Directors. In the absence or incapacity of the President, a Vice-President shall exercise the authority and perform the functions of the President.

2. A Vice-President may participate in meetings of the Board of Directors but shall have no vote at such meetings, except that

he or she may cast the deciding vote when acting in place of the President.

Article 32

INTERNATIONAL CHARACTER OF THE BANK

1. The Bank shall not accept Special Funds or other loans or assistance that may in any way prejudice, deflect or otherwise alter its purpose or functions.

2. The Bank, its President, Vice-President (s), officers and staff shall in their decisions take into account only considerations relevant to the Bank's purpose, functions and operations, as set out in this Agreement. Such considerations shall be weighed impartially in order to achieve and carry out the purpose and functions of the Bank.

3. The President, Vice-President (s), officers and staff of the Bank, in the discharge of their offices, shall owe their duty entirely to the Bank and to no other authority. Each member of the Bank shall respect the international character of this duty and shall refrain from all attempts to influence any of them in the discharge of their duties.

Article 33

LOCATION OF OFFICES

1. The principal office of the Bank shall be located in London.

2. The Bank may establish agencies or branch offices in the territory of any member of the Bank.

Article 34

DEPOSITORIES AND CHANNELS OF COMMUNICATION

1. Each member shall designate its central bank, or such other institution as may be agreed upon with the Bank, as a depository for all the Bank's holdings of its currency as well as other assets of the Bank.

2. Each member shall designate an appropriate official entity with which the Bank may communicate in connection with any matter arising under this Agreement.

Article 35

PUBLICATION OF REPORTS AND PROVISION OF INFORMATION

1. The Bank shall publish an annual report containing an audited statement of its accounts and shall circulate to members at intervals of three (3) months or less a summary statement of its financial position and a profit and loss statement showing the results of its operations. The financial accounts shall be kept in ECU.

2. The Bank shall report annually on the environmental impact of its activities and may publish such other reports as it deems desirable to advance its purpose.

3. Copies of all reports, statements and publications made under this Article shall be distributed to members.

Article 36

ALLOCATION AND DISTRIBUTION OF NET INCOME

1. The Board of Governors shall determine at least annually what part of the Bank's net income, after making provision for reserves and, if necessary, against possible losses under paragraph 1 of Article 17 of this Agreement, shall be allocated to surplus or other purposes and what part, if any, shall be distributed. Any such decision on the allocation of the Bank's net income to other purposes shall be taken by a majority of not less than two-thirds of the Governors, representing not less than two-thirds of the total voting power of the members. No such allocation, and no distribution, shall be made until the general reserve amounts to at least ten (10) per cent of the authorized capital stock.

2. Any distribution referred to in the preceding paragraph shall be made in proportion to the number of paid-in shares held by each member; provided that in calculating such number ac-

count shall be taken only of payments received in cash and promissory notes encashed in respect of such shares on or before the end of the relevant financial year.

3. Payments to each member shall be made in such manner as the Board of Governors shall determine. Such payments and their use by the receiving country shall be without restriction by any member.

Chapter VII

WITHDRAWAL AND SUSPENSION OF MEMBERSHIP: TEMPORARY SUSPENSION AND TERMINATION OF OPERATIONS

Article 37

RIGHT OF MEMBERS TO WITHDRAW

1. Any member may withdraw from the Bank at any time by transmitting a notice in writing to the Bank at its principal office.

2. Withdrawal by a member shall become effective, and its membership shall cease, on the date specified in its notice but in no event less than six (6) months after such notice is received by the Bank. However, at any time before the withdrawal becomes finally effective, the member may notify the Bank in writing of the cancellation of its notice of intention to withdraw.

Article 38

SUSPENSION OF MEMBERSHIP

1. If a member fails to fulfil any of its obligations to the Bank, the Bank may suspend its membership by decision of a majority of not less than two-thirds of the Governors, representing not less than two-thirds of the total voting power of the members. The member so suspended shall automatically cease to be a member one year from the date of its suspension unless a decision is taken by not less than the same majority to restore the member to good standing.

2. While under suspension, a member shall not be entitled to exercise any rights under this Agreement, except the right of withdrawal, but shall remain subject to all its obligations.

Article 39

SETTLEMENT OF ACCOUNTS WITH FORMER MEMBERS

1. After the date on which a member ceases to be a member, such former member shall remain liable for its direct obligations to the Bank and for its contingent liabilities to the Bank so long as any part of the loans, equity investments or guarantees contracted before it ceased to be a member are outstanding; but it shall cease to incur such liabilities with respect to loans, equity investments and guarantees entered into thereafter by the Bank and to share either in the income or the expenses of the Bank.

2. At the time a member ceases to be a member, the Bank shall arrange for the repurchase of such former member's shares as a part of the settlement of accounts with such former member in accordance with the provisions of this Article. For this purpose, the repurchase price of the shares shall be the value shown by the books of the Bank on the date of cessation of membership, with the original purchase price of each share being its maximum value.

3. The payment for shares repurchased by the Bank under this Article shall be governed by the following conditions:

(i) any amount due to the former member for its shares shall be withheld so long as the former member, its central bank or any of its agencies or instrumentalities remains liable, as borrower or guarantor, to the Bank and such amount may, at the option of the Bank, be applied on any such liability as it matures. No amount shall be withheld on account of the liability of the former member resulting from its subscription for shares in accordance with paragraphs 4, 5 and 7 of Article 6 of this Agreement. In any event, no amount due to a member for its shares shall be paid until six (6) months after the date upon which the member ceases to be a member;

(ii) payments for shares may be made from time to time, upon their surrender by the former member, to the extent by which the amount due as the repurchase price in accordance with paragraph 2 of this Article exceeds the aggregate amount of liabilities on loans, equity investments and guarantees in subparagraph (i) of this paragraph until the former member has received the full repurchase price;

(iii) payments shall be made on such conditions and in such fully convertible currencies, or ECU, and on such dates, as the Bank determines; and

(iv) if losses are sustained by the Bank on any guarantees, participations in loans, or loans which were outstanding on the date when the member ceased to be a member, or if a net loss is sustained by the Bank on equity investments held by it on such date, and the amount of such losses exceeds the amount of the reserves provided against losses on the date when the member ceased to be a member, such former member shall repay, upon demand, the amount by which the repurchase price of its shares would have been reduced if the losses had been taken into account when the repurchase price was determined. In addition, the former member shall remain liable on any call for unpaid subscriptions under paragraph 4 of Article 6 of this Agreement, to the extent that it would have been required to respond if the impairment of capital had occurred and the call had been made at the time the repurchase price of its shares was determined.

4. If the Bank terminates its operations pursuant to Article 41 of this Agreement within six (6) months of the date upon which any member ceases to be a member, all rights of such former member shall be determined in accordance with the provisions of Articles 41 to 43 of this Agreement.

Article 40

TEMPORARY SUSPENSION OF OPERATIONS

In an emergency, the Board of Directors may suspend temporarily operations in respect of new loans, guarantees, underwriting, technical assistance and equity investments pending an opportunity for further consideration and action by the Board of Governors.

Article 41

TERMINATION OF OPERATIONS

The Bank may terminate its operations by the affirmative vote of not less than two-thirds of the Governors, representing not less than three-fourths of the total voting power of the members. Upon such termination of operations the Bank shall forthwith cease all activities, except those incident to the orderly realization, conservation and preservation of its assets and settlement of its obligations.

Article 42

LIABILITY OF MEMBERS AND PAYMENT OF CLAIMS

1. In the event of termination of the operations of the Bank, the liability of all members for uncalled subscriptions to the capital stock of the Bank shall continue until all claims of creditors, including all contingent claims, shall have been discharged.

2. Creditors on ordinary operations holding direct claims shall be paid first out of the assets of the Bank, secondly out of the payments to be made to the Bank in respect of unpaid paid-in shares, and then out of payments to be made to the Bank in respect of callable capital stock. Before making any payments to creditors holding direct claims, the Board of Directors shall make such arrangements as are necessary, in its judgment, to ensure a *pro rata* distribution among holders of direct and holders of contingent claims.

Article 43

DISTRIBUTION OF ASSETS

1. No distribution under this Chapter shall be made to members on account of their subscriptions to the capital stock of the Bank until:

(i) all liabilities to creditors have been discharged or provided for; and
(ii) the Board of Governors has decided by a vote of not less than two-thirds of the Governors, representing not less than three-fourths of the total voting power of the members, to make a distribution.

2. Any distribution of the assets of the Bank to the members shall be in proportion to the capital stock held by each member and shall be effected at such times and under such conditions as the Bank shall deem fair and equitable. The shares of assets distributed need not be uniform as to type of assets. No member shall be entitled to receive its share in such a distribution of assets until it has settled all of its obligations to the Bank.

3. Any member receiving assets distributed pursuant to this Article shall enjoy the same rights with respect to such assets as the Bank enjoyed prior to their distribution.

Chapter VIII

STATUS, IMMUNITIES, PRIVILEGES AND EXEMPTIONS

Article 44

PURPOSES OF CHAPTER

To enable the Bank to fulfil its purpose and the functions with which it is entrusted, the status, immunities, privileges and exemptions set forth in this Chapter shall be accorded to the Bank in the territory of each member country.

Article 45

STATUS OF THE BANK

The Bank shall possess full legal personality and, in particular, the full legal capacity:

(i) to contract;
(ii) to acquire, and dispose of, immovable and movable property; and
(iii) to institute legal proceedings.

Article 46

POSITION OF THE BANK WITH REGARD TO JUDICIAL PROCESS

Actions may be brought against the Bank only in a court of competent jurisdiction in the territory of a country in which the Bank has an office, has appointed an agent for the purpose of accepting service or notice of process, or has issued or guaranteed securities. No actions shall, however, be brought by members or persons acting for or deriving claims from members. The property and assets of the Bank shall, wheresoever located and by whomsoever held, be immune from all forms of seizure, attachment or execution before the delivery of final judgment against the Bank.

Article 47

IMMUNITY OF ASSETS FROM SEIZURE

Property and assets of the Bank, wheresoever located and by whomsoever held, shall be immune from search, requisition, confiscation, expropriation or any other form of taking or foreclosure by executive or legislative action.

Article 48

IMMUNITY OF ARCHIVES

The archives of the Bank, and in general all documents belonging to it or held by it, shall be inviolable.

Article 49

FREEDOM OF ASSETS FROM RESTRICTIONS

To the extent necessary to carry out the purpose and functions of the Bank and subject to the provisions of this Agreement, all property and assets of the Bank shall be free from restrictions, regulations, controls and moratoria of any nature.

Article 50

PRIVILEGE FOR COMMUNICATIONS

The official communications of the Bank shall be accorded by each member the same treatment that it accords to the official communications of any other member.

Article 51

IMMUNITIES OF OFFICERS AND EMPLOYEES

All Governors, Directors, Alternates, officers and employees of the Bank and experts performing missions for the Bank shall be immune from legal process with respect to acts performed by them in their official capacity, except when the Bank waives this immunity, and shall enjoy inviolability of all their official papers and documents. This immunity shall not apply, however, to civil liability in the case of damage arising from a road traffic accident caused by any such Governor, Director, Alternate, officer, employee or expert.

Article 52

PRIVILEGES OF OFFICERS AND EMPLOYEES

1. All Governors, Directors, Alternates, officers and employees of the Bank and experts of the Bank performing missions for the Bank:

   (i) not being local nationals, shall be accorded the same immunities from immigration restrictions, alien registration requirements and national service obligations, and the same facilities as regards exchange regulations, as are accorded by members to the representatives, officials, and employees of comparable rank of other members; and

(ii) shall be granted the same treatment in respect of travelling facilities as is accorded by members to representatives, officials and employees of comparable rank of other members.

2. The spouses and immediate dependents of those Directors, Alternate Directors, officers, employees and experts of the Bank who are resident in the country in which the principal office of the Bank is located shall be accorded opportunity to take employment in that country. The spouses and immediate dependents of those Directors, Alternate Directors, officers, employees and experts of the Bank who are resident in a country in which any agency or branch office of the Bank is located should, wherever possible, in accordance with the national law of that country, be accorded similar opportunity in that country. The Bank shall negotiate specific agreements implementing the provisions of this paragraph with the country in which the principal office of the Bank is located and, as appropriate, with the other countries concerned.

Article 53

EXEMPTION FROM TAXATION

1. Within the scope of its official activities the Bank, its assets, property, and income shall be exempt from all direct taxes.

2. When purchases or services of substantial value and necessary for the exercise of the official activities of the Bank are made or used by the Bank and when the price of such purchases or services includes taxes or duties, the member that has levied the taxes or duties shall, if they are identifiable, take appropriate measures to grant exemption from such taxes or duties or to provide for their reimbursement.

3. Goods imported by the Bank and necessary for the exercise of its official activities shall be exempt from all import duties and

taxes, and from all import prohibitions and restrictions. Similarly goods exported by the Bank and necessary for the exercise of its official activities shall be exempt from all export duties and taxes, and from all export prohibitions and restrictions.

4. Goods acquired or imported and exempted under this Article shall not be sold, hired out, lent or given away against payment or free of charge, except in accordance with conditions laid down by the members which have granted exemptions or reimbursements.

5. The provisions of this Article shall not apply to taxes or duties which are no more than charges for public utility services.

6. Directors, Alternate Directors, officers and employees of the Bank shall be subject to an internal effective tax for the benefit of the Bank on salaries and emoluments paid by the Bank, subject to conditions to be laid down and rules to be adopted by the Board of Governors within a period of one year from the date of entry into force of this Agreement. From the date on which this tax is applied, such salaries and emoluments shall be exempt from national income tax. The members may, however, take into account the salaries and emoluments thus exempt when assessing the amount of tax to be applied to income from other sources.

7. Notwithstanding the provisions of paragraph 6 of this Article, a member may deposit, with its instrument of ratification, acceptance or approval, a declaration that such member retains for itself, its political subdivisions or its local authorities the right to tax salaries and emoluments paid by the Bank to citizens or nationals of such member. The Bank shall be exempt from any obligations for the payment, withholding or collection of such taxes. The Bank shall not make any reimbursement for such taxes.

8. Paragraph 6 of this Article shall not apply to pensions and annuities paid by the Bank.

9. No tax of any kind shall be levied on any obligation or security issued by the Bank, including any dividend or interest thereon, by whomsoever held:

(i) which discriminates against such obligation or security solely because it is issued by the Bank, or

(ii) if the sole jurisdictional basis for such taxation is the place or currency in which it is issued, made payable or paid, or the location of any office or place of business maintained by the Bank.

10. No tax of any kind shall be levied on any obligation or security guaranteed by the Bank, including any dividend or interest thereon by whomsoever held:

(i) which discriminates against such obligation or security solely because it is guaranteed by the Bank, or

(ii) if the sole jurisdictional basis for such taxation is the location of any office or place of business maintained by the Bank.

Article 54

IMPLEMENTATION OF CHAPTER

Each member shall promptly take such action as is necessary for the purpose of implementing the provisions of this Chapter and shall inform the Bank of the detailed action which it has taken.

Article 55

WAIVER OF IMMUNITIES, PRIVILEGES AND EXEMPTIONS

The immunities, privileges and exemptions conferred under this Chapter are granted in the interest of the Bank. The Board of Directors may waive to such extent and upon such conditions as it may determine any of the immunities, privileges and exemptions conferred under this Chapter in cases where such action would, in its opinion, be appropriate in the best interests of the Bank. The President shall have the right and the duty to waive any immunity, privilege or exemption in respect of any officer, employee or expert of the Bank, other than the President or a Vice-President, where, in his or her opinion, the immunity, privilege or exemption would impede the course of justice and can be waived without prejudice to the interests of the Bank. In similar circumstances and under the same conditions, the Board of Directors shall have the right and the duty to waive any immunity, privilege or exemption in respect of the President and each Vice-President.

Chapter IX

AMENDMENTS, INTERPRETATION, ARBITRATION

Article 56

AMENDMENTS

1. Any proposals to amend this Agreement, whether emanating from a member, a Governor or the Board of Directors, shall be communicated to the Chairman of the Board of Governors who shall bring the proposal before the Board. If the proposed amendment is approved by the Board the Bank shall, by any rapid means of communication, ask all members whether they accept the proposed amendment. When not less than three-fourths of the members (including at least two countries from Central and Eastern Europe listed in Annex A), having not less than four-fifths of the total voting power of the members, have accepted the proposed amendment, the Bank shall certify that fact by formal communication addressed to all members.

2. Notwithstanding paragraph 1 of this Article:

(i) acceptance by all members shall be required in the case of any amendment modifying:
   (a) the right to withdraw from the Bank;
   (b) the rights pertaining to purchase of capital stock provided for in paragraph 3 of Article 5 of this Agreement;
   (c) the limitation on liability provided for in paragraph 7 of Article 5 of this Agreement; and
   (d) the purpose and functions of the Bank defined by Articles 1 and 2 of this Agreement;

(ii) acceptance by not less than three-fourths of the members having not less than eighty-five (85) percent of the total voting power of the members shall be required in the case of any amendment modifying paragraph 4 of Article 8 of this Agreement.

When the requirements for accepting any such proposed amendment have been met, the Bank shall certify that fact by formal communication addressed to all members.

3. Amendments shall enter into force for all members three (3) months after the date of the formal communication provided for in paragraphs 1 and 2 of this Article unless the Board of Governors specifies a different period.

Article 57

INTERPRETATION AND APPLICATION

1. Any question of interpretation or application of the provisions of this Agreement arising between any member and the Bank, or between any members of the Bank, shall be submitted to the Board of Directors for its decision. If there is no Director of its nationality in that Board, a member particularly affected by the question under consideration shall be entitled to direct representation in the meeting of the Board of Directors during such consideration. The representative of such member shall, however, have no vote. Such right of representation shall be regulated by the Board of Governors.

2. In any case where the Board of Directors has given a decision under paragraph 1 of this Article, any member may require that the question be referred to the Board of Governors, whose decision shall be final. Pending the decision of the Board of Governors, the Bank may, so far as it deems it necessary, act on the basis of the decision of the Board of Directors.

Article 58

ARBITRATION

If a disagreement should arise between the Bank and a member which has ceased to be a member, or between the Bank and any member after adoption of a decision to terminate the operations of the Bank, such disagreement shall be submitted to arbitration by a tribunal of three (3) arbitrators, one appointed by the Bank, another by the member or former member concerned, and the third, unless the parties otherwise agree, by the President of the International Court of Justice or such other authority as may have been prescribed by regulations adopted by the Board of Governors. A majority vote of the arbitrators shall be sufficient to reach a decision which shall be final and binding upon the parties. The third arbitrator shall have full power to settle all questions of procedure in any case where the parties are in disagreement with respect thereto.

Article 59

APPROVAL DEEMED GIVEN

Whenever the approval or the acceptance of any member is required before any act may be done by the Bank, except under Article 56 of this Agreement, approval or acceptance shall be deemed to have been given unless the member presents an objection within such reasonable period as the Bank may fix in notifying the member of the proposed act.

Chapter X

FINAL PROVISION

Article 60

SIGNATURE AND DEPOSIT

1. This Agreement, deposited with the Government of the French Republic (hereinafter called "the Depository"), shall remain open until 31 December 1990 for signature by the prospective members whose names are set forth in Annex A to this Agreement.
2. The Depository shall communicate certified copies of this Agreement to all the Signatories.

Article 61

RATIFICATION, ACCEPTANCE OR APPROVAL

1. The Agreement shall be subject to ratification, acceptance or approval by the Signatories. Instruments of ratification, acceptance or approval shall, subject to paragraph 2 of this Article, be deposited with the Depository not later than 31 March 1991. The Depository shall duly notify the other Signatories of each deposit and the date thereof.

2. Any Signatories may become a party to this Agreement by depositing an instrument of ratification, acceptance or approval until one year after the date of its entry into force or, if necessary, until such later date as may be decided by a majority of Governors, representing a majority of the total voting power of the members.

3. A Signatory whose instrument referred to in paragraph 1 of this Article is deposited before the date on which this Agreement enters into force shall become a member of the Bank on that date. Any other Signatory which complies with the provisions of the preceding paragraph shall become a member of the Bank on the date on which its instrument of ratification, acceptance or approval is deposited.

Article 62

ENTRY INTO FORCE

1. This Agreement shall enter into force when instruments of ratification, acceptance or approval have been deposited by Signatories whose initial subscriptions represent not less than two-thirds of the total subscriptions set forth in Annex A, including at least two countries from Central and Eastern Europe listed in Annex A.

2. If this Agreement has not entered into force by 31 March 1991, the Depository may convene a conference of interested prospective members to determine the future course of action and decide a new date by which instruments of ratification, acceptance or approval shall be deposited.

Article 63

INAUGURAL MEETING AND COMMENCEMENT OF OPERATIONS

1. As soon as this Agreement enters into force under Article 62 of this Agreement, each member shall appoint a Governor. The Depository shall call the first meeting of the Board of Governors within sixty (60) days of entry into force of this Agreement under Article 62 or as soon as possible thereafter.

2. At its first meeting, the Board of Governors:

(i) shall elect the President;
(ii) shall elect the Directors of the Bank in accordance with Article 26 of this Agreement;
(iii) shall make arrangements for determining the date of the commencement of the Bank's operations; and
(iv) shall make such other arrangements as appear to it necessary to prepare for the commencement of the Bank's operations.

3. The Bank shall notify its members of the date of commencement of its operations.

Done at Paris on 29 May 1990 in a single original, whose English, French, German and Russian texts are equally authentic, which shall be deposited in the archives of the Depository which shall transmit a duly certified copy to each of the other prospective members whose names are set forth in Annex A.

Appendix II

ANNEX A [of the Agreement]

INITIAL SUBSCRIPTIONS TO THE AUTHORIZED CAPITAL STOCK FOR PROSPECTIVE MEMBERS WHICH MAY BECOME MEMBERS IN ACCORDANCE WITH ARTICLE 61

			Number of Shares	Capital Subscription (in million ECUs)
A.	Members of the European Communities			
	(a)	Belgium	22,800	228.00
		Denmark	12,000	120.00
		France	85,175	851.75
		Germany, Federal Republic of	85,175	851.75
		Greece	6,500	65.00
		Ireland	3,000	30.00
		Italy	85,175	851.75
		Luxembourg	2,000	20.00
		Netherlands	24,800	248.00
		Portugal	4,200	42.00
		Spain	34,000	340.00
		United Kingdom	85,175	851.75
	(b)	European Economic Community	30,000	300.00
		European Investment Bank	30,000	300.00
B.	Other European Countries			
		Austria	22,800	228.00
		Cyprus	1,000	10.00
		Finland	12,500	125.00

	Number of Shares	Capital Subscription (in million ECUs)
Iceland	1,000	10.00
Israel	6,500	65.00
Liechtenstein	200	2.00
Malta	100	1.00
Norway	12,500	125.00
Sweden	22,800	228.00
Switzerland	22,800	228.00
Turkey	11,500	115.00
C. Recipient Countries		
Bulgaria	7,900	79.00
Czechoslovakia	12,800	128.00
German Democratic Republic	15,500	155.00
Hungary	7,900	79.00
Poland	12,800	128.00
Romania	4,800	48.00
Union of Soviet Socialist Republics	60,000	600.00
Yugoslavia	12,800	128.00
D. Non-European Countries		
Australia	10,000	100.00
Canada	34,000	340.00
Egypt	1,000	10.00
Japan	85,175	851.75
Korea, Republic of	6,500	65.00
Mexico	3,000	30.00
Morocco	1,000	10.00
New Zealand	1,000	10.00
United States of America	100,000	1,000.00
E. Non-allocated shares		
TOTAL	125 1,000,000	1.25 10,000.00

(*)Prospective members are listed under the above categories only for the purpose of this Agreement. Recipient countries are referred to elsewhere in this Agreement as Central and Eastern European countries.

Appendix III

ANNEX B [of the Agreement]

SECTION A - ELECTION OF DIRECTORS BY GOVERNORS REPRESENTING BELGIUM, DENMARK, FRANCE, THE FEDERAL REPUBLIC OF GERMANY, GREECE, IRELAND, ITALY, LUXEMBOURG, THE NETHERLANDS, PORTUGAL, SPAIN, THE UNITED KINGDOM, THE EUROPEAN ECONOMIC COMMUNITY AND THE EUROPEAN INVESTMENT BANK (HEREINAFTER REFERRED TO AS SECTION A GOVERNORS).

1. The provisions set out below in this Section shall apply exclusively to this Section.

2. Candidates for the office of Director shall be nominated by Section A Governors, provided that a Governor may nominate only one person. The election of Directors shall be by ballot of Section A Governors.

3. Each Governor eligible to vote shall cast for one person all of the votes to which the member appointing him or her is entitled under paragraphs 1 and 2 of Article 29 of this Agreement.

4. Subject to paragraph 10 of this Section, the 11 persons receiving the highest number of votes shall be Directors, except that no person who received less than 4.5 per cent of the total of the votes which can be cast (eligible votes) in Section A shall be considered elected.

5. Subject to paragraph 10 of this Section, if 11 persons are not elected on the first ballot, a second ballot shall be held in which, unless there were no more than 11 candidates, the person who received the lowest number of votes in the first ballot shall be ineligible for election and in which there shall vote only:

(a) those Governors who voted in the first ballot for a person not elected; and
(b) those Governors whose votes for a person elected are deemed under paragraphs 6 and 7 below of this Section to have raised the votes cast for that person above 5.5 per cent of the eligible votes.

6. In determining whether the votes cast by a Governor are deemed to have raised the total votes cast for any person above 5.5 per cent of the eligible votes, the 5.5 per cent shall be deemed to include, first, the votes of the Governor casting the largest number of votes for such person, then the votes of the Governor casting the next largest number and so on, until 5.5 per cent is reached.

7. Any Governor, part of whose votes must be counted in order to raise the total of votes cast for any person above 4.5 per cent shall be considered as casting all of his or her votes for such person, even if the total votes for such person thereby exceed 5.5 per cent and shall not be eligible to vote in a further ballot.

8. Subject to paragraph 10 of this Section, if, after the second ballot, 11 persons have not been elected, further ballots shall be held in conformity with the principles and procedures laid down in this Section, until 11 persons have been elected, provided that, if at any stage 10 persons are elected, notwithstanding the provisions of paragraph 4 of this Section, the 11th may be elected by a simple majority of the remaining votes cast.

9. In the case of an increase or decrease in the number of Directors to be elected by Section A Governors, the minimum and maximum percentages specified in paragraphs 4, 5, 6 and 7 of this Section shall be appropriately adjusted by the Board of Governors.

10. So long as any Signatory, or group of Signatories, whose share of the total amount of capital subscriptions provided in Annex A is more than 2.4 per cent, has not deposited its instrument or their instruments of ratification, approval or acceptance, there shall be no election for one Director in respect of each such Signatory or group of Signatories. The Governor or Governors representing such a Signatory or group of Signatories shall elect a Director in respect of each Signatory or group of Signatories, immediately after the Signatory becomes a member or the group

of Signatories become members. Such Director shall be deemed to have been elected by the Board of Governors at its inaugural meeting, in accordance with paragraph 3 of Article 26 of this Agreement, if he or she is elected during the period in which the first Board of Directors shall hold office.

SECTION B - ELECTION OF DIRECTORS BY GOVERNORS REPRESENTING OTHER COUNTRIES

Section B (i) - Election of Directors by Governors representing those countries listed in Annex A as Central and Eastern European Countries (recipient countries) (hereinafter referred to as Section B (i) Governors).

1. The provisions set out below in this Section shall apply exclusively to this Section.

2. Candidates for the office of Director shall be nominated by Section B (i) Governors, provided that a Governor may nominate only one person. The election of Directors shall be by ballot of Section B (i) Governors.

3. Each Governor eligible to vote shall cast for one person all of the votes to which the member appointing him or her is entitled under paragraphs 1 and 2 of Article 29 of this Agreement.

4. Subject to paragraph 10 of this Section, the 4 persons receiving the highest number of votes shall be Directors, except that no person who receives less than 12 per cent of the total of the votes which can be cast (eligible votes) in Section B (i) shall be considered elected.

5. Subject to paragraph 10 of this Section, if 4 persons are not elected on the first ballot, a second ballot shall be held in which, unless there were no more than 4 candidates, the person who received the lowest number of votes in the first ballot shall be ineligible for election and in which there shall vote only:

(a) those Governors who voted in the first ballot for a person not elected; and
(b) those Governors whose votes for a person elected are deemed under paragraphs 6 and 7 below of this Section to have raised the votes cast for that person above 13 per cent of the eligible votes.

6. In determining whether the votes cast by a Governor are deemed to have raised the total votes cast for any person above 13 per cent of the eligible votes, the 13 per cent shall be deemed to include, first, the votes of the Governor casting the largest number of votes for such person, then the votes of the Governor casting the next largest number and so on, until 13 per cent is reached.

7. Any Governor, part of whose votes must be counted in order to raise the total of votes cast for any person above 12 per cent shall be considered as casting all of his or her votes for such person, even if the total votes for such person thereby exceed 13 per cent and shall not be eligible to vote in a further ballot.

8. Subject to paragraph 10 of this Section, if, after the second ballot, 4 persons have not been elected, further ballots shall be held in conformity with the principles and procedures laid down in this Section, until 4 persons have been elected, provided that, if at any stage 3 persons are elected, notwithstanding the provisions of paragraph 4 of this Section, the 4th may be elected by a simple majority of the remaining votes cast.

9. In the case of an increase or decrease in the number of Directors to be elected by Section B (i) Governors, the minimum and maximum percentages specified in paragraphs 4, 5, 6 and 7 of this Section shall be appropriately adjusted by the Board of Governors.

10. So long as any Signatory, or group of Signatories, whose share of the total amount of capital subscriptions provided in Annex A is more than 2.8 per cent, has not deposited its instrument or their instruments of ratification, approval or acceptance, there shall be no election for one Director in respect of each such Signatory or group of Signatories. The Governor or Governors representing such a Signatory or group of Signatories shall elect a Director in respect of each Signatory or group of Signatories, immediately after the Signatory becomes a member or the group of Signatories become members. Such Director shall be deemed to have been elected by the Board of Governors at its inaugural meeting, in accordance with paragraph 3 of Article 26 of this Agreement, if he or she is elected during the period in which the first Board of Directors shall hold office.

Section B (ii) - Election of Directors by Governor representing those countries listed in Annex A as other European countries (hereinafter referred to as Section B (ii) Governors).

1. The provision set out below in this Section shall apply exclusively to this Section.

2. Candidates for the office of Director shall be nominated by Section B (ii) Governors, provided that a Governor may nominate only one person. The election of Directors shall be by ballot of Section B (ii) Governors.

3. Each Governor eligible to vote shall cast for one person all of the votes to which the member appointing him or her is entitled under paragraphs 1 and 2 of Article 29 of this Agreement.

4. Subject to paragraph 10 of this Section, the 4 persons receiving the highest number of votes shall be Directors, except that no person who receives less than 20.5 per cent of the votes which can be cast (eligible votes) in Section B (ii) shall be considered elected.

5. Subject to paragraph 10 of this Section, if 4 persons are not elected on the first ballot, a second ballot shall be held in which, unless there were no more than 4 candidates, the person who received the lowest number of votes in the first ballot shall be ineligible for election and in which there shall vote only:

- (a) those Governors who voted in the first ballot for a person not elected; and
- (b) those Governors whose vote for a person elected are deemed under paragraphs 6 and 7 below of this Section to have raised the votes cast for that person above 21.5 per cent of the eligible votes.

6. In determining whether the votes cast by a Governor are deemed to have raised the total votes cast for any person above 21.5 per cent of the eligible votes, the 21.5 per cent shall be deemed to include, first, the votes of the Governor casting the largest number of votes for such person, then the votes of the Governor casting the next largest number and so on, until 21.5 per cent is reached.

7. Any Governor, part of whose votes must be counted in order to raise the total of votes cast for any person above 20.5 per cent shall be considered as casting all of his or her votes for such person, even if the total votes for such person thereby exceed 21.5 per cent and shall not be eligible to vote in a further ballot.

8. Subject to paragraph 10 of this Section, if, after the second ballot, 4 persons have not been elected, further ballots shall be held in conformity with the principles and procedures laid down in this Section, until 4 persons have been elected, provided that, if at any stage 3 persons are elected, notwithstanding the provisions of paragraph 4 of this Section, the 4th may be elected by a simple majority of the remaining votes cast.

9. In the case of an increase or decrease in the number of Directors to be elected by Section B (ii) Governors, the minimum and maximum percentages specified in paragraphs 4, 5, 6 and 7 of this Section shall be appropriately adjusted by the Board of Governors.

10. So long as any Signatory, or group of Signatories, whose share of the total amount of capital subscriptions provided in Annex A is more than 2.8 per cent, has not deposited its instrument or their instruments of ratification, approval or acceptance, there shall be no election for one Director in respect of each such Signatory or group of Signatories. The Governor or Governors representing such a Signatory or group of Signatories shall elect a Director in respect of each Signatory or group of Signatories, immediately after the Signatory becomes a member or the group of Signatories become members. Such Director shall be deemed to have been elected by the Board of Governors at its inaugural meeting, in accordance with paragraph 3 of Article 26 of this Agreement, if he or she is elected during the period in which the first Board of Directors shall hold office.

Section B (iii) - Election of Directors by Governors Representing those Countries Listed in Annex A as Non-European Countries (hereinafter referred to as Section B (iii) Governors).

1. The provisions set out below in this Section shall apply exclusively to this Section.

2. Candidates for the office of Director shall be nominated by Section B (iii) Governors, provided that a Governor may nominate only one person. The election of Directors shall be by ballot of Section B (iii) Governors.

3. Each Governor eligible to vote shall cast for one person all of the votes to which the member appointing him or her is entitled under paragraphs 1 and 2 of Article 29 of this Agreement.

4. Subject to paragraph 10 of this Section, the 4 persons receiving the highest number of votes shall be Directors, except that no person who receives less than 8 per cent of the total of the votes which can be cast (eligible votes) in Section B (iii) shall be considered elected.

5. Subject to paragraph 10 of this Section, if 4 persons are not elected on the first ballot, a second ballot shall be held in which, unless there were no more than 4 candidates, the person who received the lowest number of votes in the first ballot shall be ineligible for election and in which there shall vote only:

(a) those Governors who voted in the first ballot for a person not elected; and
(b) those Governors whose votes for a person elected are deemed under paragraphs 6 and 7 below of this Section to have raised the votes cast for that person above 9 per cent of the eligible votes.

6. In determining whether the votes cast by a Governor are deemed to have raised the total votes cast for any person above 9 per cent of the eligible votes, the 9 per cent shall be deemed to include, first, the votes of the Governor casting the largest number of votes for such person, then the votes of the Governor casting the next largest number and so on, until 9 per cent is reached.

7. Any Governor, part of whose votes must be counted in order to raise the total of votes cast for any person above 8 per cent shall be considered as casting all of his or her votes for such person, even if the total votes for such person thereby exceed 9 per cent and shall not be eligible to vote in a further ballot.

8. Subject to paragraph 10 of this Section, if, after the second ballot, 4 persons have not been elected, further ballots shall be held in conformity with the principles and procedures laid down in this Section, until 4 persons have been elected, provided that,

if at any stage 3 persons are elected, notwithstanding the provisions of paragraph 4 of this Section, the 4th may be elected by a simple majority of the remaining votes cast.

9. In the case of an increase or decrease in the number of Directors to be elected by Section B (iii) Governors, the minimum and maximum percentages specified in paragraph 4, 5, 6 and 7 of this Section shall be appropriately adjusted by the Board of Governors.

10. So long as any Signatory, or group of Signatories, whose share of the total amount of capital subscriptions provided in Annex A is more than 5 per cent, has not deposited its instrument or their instruments of ratification, approval or acceptance, there shall be no election for one Director in respect of each such Signatory or group of Signatories. The Governor or Governors representing such a Signatory or group of Signatories shall elect a Director in respect of each Signatory or group of Signatories, immediately after the Signatory becomes a member or the group of Signatories become members. Such Director shall be deemed to have been elected by the Board of Governors at its inaugural meeting, in accordance with paragraph 3 of Article 26 of this Agreement, if he or she is elected during the period in which the first Board of Directors shall hold office.

SECTION C - ARRANGEMENTS FOR THE ELECTION OF DIRECTORS REPRESENTING COUNTRIES NOT LISTED IN ANNEX A.

If the Board of Governors decides, in accordance with paragraph 3 of Article 26 of this Agreement, to increase or decrease the size, or revise the composition, of the Board of Directors, in order to take into account changes in the number of members of the Bank, the Board of Governors shall first consider whether any amendments are required to this Annex, and may make any such amendments as it deems necessary as part of such decision.

SECTION D - ASSIGNMENT OF VOTES

Any Governor who does not participate in voting for the election or whose vote does not contribute to the election of a Director under Section A or Section B (i) or Section B (ii) or Section

B (iii) of this Annex may assign the votes to which he or she is entitled to an elected Director, provided that such Governor shall first have obtained the agreement of all those Governors who have elected that Director to such assignment.

A decision by any Governor not to participate in voting for the election of a Director shall not affect the calculation of the eligible votes to be made under Section A, Section B (i), Section B (ii) or Section B (iii) of this Annex.

Appendix IV

To the Chairman of the
Conference on the
Establishment of the
European Bank for
Reconstruction and Development

Mr. Chairman,

As you know, the initiative of the President of France M. P. Mitterrand to establish the European Bank for Reconstruction and Development for the purpose of facilitating the transition of Central and Eastern European countries towards market-oriented economies has found understanding and support on behalf of the Soviet authorities. The Soviet delegation participated in the sessions of talks on drafting the constituent documents of the Bank. As a result the constituent countries have reached considerable progress in drawing up the Agreement establishing the European Bank for Reconstruction and Development.

At the same time, certain difficulties largely stem from fears of a number of countries that due to the size of its economy the Soviet Union may become the principal recipient of credits of the Bank and therefore will narrow its capacity to extend aid to other Central and Eastern European Countries.

In this connexion I would like to assure you, dear Mr. Chairman, that the intentions of the Soviet Union to become an equal member of the Bank account primarily for its will to establish a new institution of multilateral co-operation so as to foster historical reforms on the European continent.

I would like to inform you that my government is prepared to limit its access to the Bank's resources, pursuant to paragraph 4 of Article 8 of the Articles of Agreement of the Bank, for a period of three years starting from the entry into force of the Articles of Agreement of the Bank.

During that period, the Soviet Union wishes that the Bank will provide technical assistance and other types of assistance directed to finance its private sector, to facilitate the transition of state-owned enterprises to private sector ownership and control and to help enterprises operating competitively and moving to participation in the market-oriented economy, subject to the proportion set forth in paragraph 3 of Article 11 of this Agreement. The total amount of any assistance thus provided by the Bank would not exceed the total amount of the cash disbursed and the promissory notes issued by the Soviet Union for its shares.

I am confident, that continuing economic reforms in the Soviet Union will inevitably promote the expansion of the Bank's activities into the territory of the Soviet Union. However, the USSR, being interested in securing the multilateral character of the Bank, will not choose that at any time in future the Soviet borrowings will exceed an amount consistent with maintaining the necessary diversity in the bank's operations and prudent limits on its exposure.

Please accept, Mr. Chairman, the assurances of my highest consideration.

Head of Soviet Delegation
Chairman of the Board
of the State Bank of the USSR
Victor V. Gerashchenko

Appendix V

Chairman's Report on the Agreement Establishing the European Bank for Reconstruction and Development

The European Bank for Reconstruction and Development (EBRD) stems from an initiative by President Mitterrand of France, strongly endorsed by the European Council at Strasbourg on 9 December, 1989, as a positive reaction from the European Community to the dramatic political and economic changes in Central and Eastern Europe.

From the beginning it was envisaged that the meetings to discuss the setting up of the Bank would be open to other countries as well as those of Central and Eastern Europe. The first meetings of potential members took place in Paris on 15 and 16 January 1990, with representatives from all 24 members of the Organization for Economic Cooperation and Development; Malta and Cyprus; eight Central and Eastern European countries; the European Economic Community and the European Investment Bank. At meetings from 8 to 11 March, 1990, these Delegates were joined by representatives from Egypt, Israel, the Republic of Korea, Liechtenstein and Morocco and on 8 and 9 April also by representatives from Mexico. The final negotiations were in Paris on 20 May, 1990.

During the meetings to discuss the EBRD Articles, Delegates came to the view that certain formulations in the text represented general understandings which needed to be recorded, but which were not suitable for the Articles. It was therefore agreed that the Chairman would produce this report summarising these understandings and that the report would form part of the EBRD's basic documents, for future reference in interpreting the Articles. The explanatory paragraphs attached to this introduction, which form the bulk of this report, should be viewed against that background. A Signing Ceremony for the Agreement took place in Paris on 29 May, 1990, in the presence of President Mitterrand and many Ministers from countries participating in the Bank.

Explanatory Notes

ARTICLE 2

1. Delegates were anxious to show that the focus of the Bank's functions was the private sector but, given that the private sector in the potential recipient countries was at present either small or non-existent, that the Bank would also support the public sector in its transition from purely centralized control to demonopolisation, decentralisation or privatisation and to a competitive business environment, and would assist recipient member countries in implementing structural and economic reforms, only through the measures described in subparagraphs (i) to (viii) inclusive of paragraph 1 of this Article.

2. In paragraph 1, subparagraph (i), Delegates shared the view that "other interested investors" covered both domestic and foreign investors.

3. In paragraph 1, subparagraph (iii), Delegates understood that "infrastructure" might include training in managerial and technical skills.

4. In paragraph 1, subparagraph (vii), Delegates recognized the serious environmental problems in Central and Eastern Europe, and emphasized that principles of environmentally sound development must be integrated into the full range of the Bank's operations. Thus Delegates intended "in the full range of its activities" to include all of the Bank's activities, including technical assistance and all special operations, and not merely that

the Bank should be able to provide support directly for specific environmental projects.

5. In paragraph 2, Delegates believed it essential that the Bank should work in "close cooperation" with the IMF and the World Bank Group (including the IFC and MIGA), so as to ensure compatibility with their activities and to benefit from their experience and expertise, as well as to ensure that recipient member countries were pursuing sound economic programmes.

6. In continuing that the close cooperation should be "with all its members", Delegates had especially in mind the important role of the European Economic Community and the European Investment Bank.

7. In the same paragraph, Delegates also understood that "other related bodies and any entity, whether public or private" included such bodies as the Council of Europe (and in particular the Social Development Fund), the International Investment Bank, the Nordic Investment Bank and the Economic Commission for Europe. Delegates noted that the Bank was free, in accordance with paragraph 1 subparagraph (viii) of Article 20 of the Agreement, to enter into agreements of cooperation with any such body.

ARTICLE 3

1. Delegates agreed that both the European Economic Community and the European Investment Bank (E.I.B.) should be members, given the importance accorded to their role by the European Community Heads of State or Government who had first endorsed the idea of the Bank. It was not intended that their membership would be a precedent for other organisations or Banks to become members of the Bank, or that their membership would be used as a precedent for them to become members of other organizations or other banks.

2. Delegations took note that the E.I.B. and its participating members confirmed that the E.I.B. had legal power to make a capital subscription to the Bank under the Statute of the European Investment Bank.

ARTICLE 4

The essentially European character of the Bank lent itself to the denomination of its original authorised capital stock in the European Currency Unit, the ECU. Delegates understood the ECU to be at the centre of the European Monetary System and formulated in relation to a basket of European Community currencies, the weights of which are re-examined by European Community Finance Ministers every five years or, on request, if the weight of any currency has changed by 25 per cent.

ARTICLE 5

1. Paragraph 3 requires the Board of Governors to review the adequacy and composition of the Bank's capital stock at least every five years. A decision may then be taken either to increase the capital stock or not. This paragraph lays down the preemptive rights of all members in the event of an increase and stipulates that there is no obligation upon any member to subscribe to new shares. These rights are then protected by paragraph 2 of Article 56 of the Articles of Agreement.
2. Paragraph 4 provides for the possibility of decisions to allow individual members to increase their shareholding in the Bank. Where such an increase is not possible without an increase in the total capital stock, the pre-emptive rights and other requirements of paragraph 3 are brought into play.

ARTICLE 6

1. In paragraph 2, Delegates agreed that the drawdown of promissory notes should be *pro rata* based on a schedule to be established by the Board of Directors who should take account of the net financing requirement based on historical resource flows.
2. In paragraph 3, Delegates agreed that the initial choice between ECU, United States dollars or Japanese yen made by each member would apply to the payment of all of the instalments mentioned in paragraph 1, as well as to the payments made as a result of a call on the original capital.

ARTICLE 8

In relation to the implementation of paragraph 3 of this Article, Delegates understood that the same procedures and voting arrangements described in this paragraph for suspending or otherwise modifying a member's access to Bank resources should apply to the reverse circumstances, namely when a member's access to Bank resources was being reconsidered in the light of its resuming the implementation of policies consistent with Article 1 of the Agreement.

ARTICLE 11

1. This Article establishes the ways the Bank shall carry out its purpose and functions, including in relation to regional projects. In describing recipients of Bank financing and assistance, and in setting limits on Bank financing and assistance to the state sector, the Article seeks to take into account the different arrangements in the different countries.

2. Delegates emphasized, in relation to the reference to private ownership and control in this Article, that control by private investors meant the ability effectively to determine enterprise decisions and policies.

3. In paragraph 1 subparagraph (v), Delegates were aware that the infrastructure needs of the potential recipient countries were immense but also that there were existing bilateral and multilateral sources of help for that purpose. They thus deliberately limited the Bank's possible activities relating to infrastructure reconstruction and development to those "necessary for private sector development and the transition to a market-oriented economy".

4. Delegates intended that paragraph 1, subparagraph (ii) (c) of this Article would be read together with subparagraph (vii) of Article 13. The Bank was not to engage in underwriting when private sector securities firms or others were able to provide the relevant financing, services and facilities on reasonable terms.

ARTICLE 12

1. Delegates intended this Article to reinforce the financial soundness of the Bank.

2. In interpreting the meaning of "the total amount of outstanding loans, equity investments and guarantees" in paragraph 1, Delegates shared the view that the Board of Directors should exercise prudence in approving all such commitments in line with its obligations under paragraph 1 of this Article.

3. In paragraph 2, Delegates intended the Board of Directors to make a rule stipulating the maximum stake that the Bank should take in the equity of any enterprise, but that this rule should include provision for exceptions in specific circumstances where this seemed desirable or necessary. Such circumstances might, for instance arise if a financing partner decided to reduce its own stake in the relevant equity.

4. In paragraph 3, Delegates meant "disbursed equity investments" to be interpreted as excluding any such investments as might subsequently have been disposed of to the value achieved by such realization.

ARTICLE 13

1. Delegates expected that the operational principles set forth in this Article would be supplemented by a more detailed and comprehensive statement of operating policies to be adopted by the Board of Directors. This statement of policies would cover, among other things: the extent to which the Bank would be expected to go to satisfy itself that the funds which it invested were used efficiently and economically and, where such funds were used for the purchase of goods, that the goods were bought on reasonable terms and in favourable markets; and the detailed requirements for the identification, appraisal, monitoring, implementation and ex-post evaluation of all projects, including their economic, technical, managerial, financial and environmental aspects.

2. In sub-paragraph (i), the stipulation that the Bank should apply sound banking principles to all its operations was meant to cover all of its activities, including its financial policies (for example its management of exchange rate risks) and not just the activities listed in the rest of the Article.

3. In sub-paragraph (ii), Delegates described the precise form of programme lending in which the Bank could become involved as "projects, whether individual or in the context of specific

investment programmes", so as to make clear that fast-disbursing policy based lending is not included.

4. In sub-paragraph (vii), the intention of Delegates was that the Bank should not compete with other organizations; rather, it should complement or supplement existing financing possibilities. Delegates also understood that "financing" and "facilities" were broad terms involving the whole range of Bank operations, including underwriting. Delegates intended this sub-paragraph to be read together with sub-paragraph (xi), where the latter applies.

5. In sub-paragraph (x), Delegates intended the word "investments" to cover the Bank's loans and guarantees as well as its equity investments. In connection with this provision it had seemed desirable to avoid writing into the Articles any requirement that preference be given to any particular class or classes of purchasers. However, the Bank could often find it necessary or appropriate, when making an investment, to give to private investors with which it was associated in the enterprise a right of first refusal, within a reasonable time limit, to purchase the Bank's interest therein. Moreover, if the Bank had various opportunities of selling an investment on roughly the same terms, it should bear in mind, in deciding among them, the desirability of fostering local capital markets.

6. In sub-paragraph (xii), Delegates agreed upon completely open procurement (and not procurement open only to members), based on international tendering, where appropriate, and believed that such tenders should be genuinely competitive, in line with the G.A.T.T. Agreement on Government Procurement. Private sector enterprises in which the Bank held equity or debt might be encouraged, but not obliged, to use international tenders to obtain goods or services efficiently and economically. Delegates were also anxious to give less developed countries, who might not become members, the opportunity to tender for Bank contracts, on equal terms with Bank members, as a means of assisting their development process and of reassuring them, through this original gesture, that the interest of shareholders in the new Bank did not mean reduced interest in their traditional partners in development.

ARTICLE 14

1. Paragraph 1 requires the Bank, in setting terms and conditions for its financing operations, to take full account of the need to safeguard its income. Delegates envisaged that this requirement would avoid the risk of such operations being in practice subsidised from the cost-free resources available to the Bank from members' paid-in subscriptions.

2. The wording of paragraph 2 of this Article gives the Bank some flexibility to react according to circumstances and would permit the Board to consider a wide range of factors in deciding a policy on guarantees for loans to state-owned enterprises.

3. In reaching decisions on these issues, the Board would need to bear in mind that a fundamental goal of the Bank was to develop a strong private sector in eligible member countries. To ensure that private entrepreneurs took full responsibility for their commercial undertakings, the Board shall follow the present practice of the International Finance Corporation in not requiring a member government guarantee on loans to private sector enterprises. It could take into account the fact that a state-owned enterprise would be more likely to respond quickly to market forces, and to make the transition to market-oriented economies, if that enterprise could not rely on a government guarantee to discharge its responsibilities under a Bank loan. The Board could also set loan terms, pursuant to paragraph (xi) of Article 13, to compensate the Bank for any commercial or other risks should it decide not to require a guarantee by a member government.

4. For the purpose of Article 11, paragraph 3, when the Bank does require a member country guarantee to a state-owned enterprise (i.e. a guarantee by the member or a public agency or instrumentality), the loan shall be considered as made to the state sector unless that state-owned enterprise is in transition to private ownership and control. A former state-owned enterprise which has achieved private ownership and control shall be regarded as a private sector enterprise, and the Bank shall not require member country guarantees on new loans to that enterprise.

ARTICLE 17

Delegates made no provision in respect of possible losses arising on special operations. Delegates envisaged that the Bank would make specific arrangements with the source of each relevant Special Fund in the agreement governing its use, so as to protect the separation of each type of resource in accordance with paragraph 2 of Article 10.

ARTICLE 18

Delegates understood that Special Funds accepted by the Bank would be assets of the Bank for the purposes of the privileges and immunities provisions of the Articles. Delegates envisaged that each Special Fund would be used and accounted for separately, but this was not specified since it was a matter for the source of each such Fund to determine in consultation with the Bank.

ARTICLE 20

1. In giving the Bank the general power to underwrite under this Article, Delegates had in mind that the Bank could agree to take on to its own books, if necessary and for a commission, some agreed portion of any shares and securities unsold as a result of a public or private enterprise issuing equity share capital or securities. If the issue proved a complete success such shares or securities would not need to be taken up by the Bank. If some remained unsold, however, and if the Bank's underwriting commitment was invoked, such shares and securities would then form part of the Bank's overall exposure in the country concerned and be subject to any limits applicable.

2. Delegates agreed that underwriting should only represent a small part of the Bank's activities, in view of the financial risks involved; that the Bank should only undertake underwriting services when necessary to fill market gaps; and that the general power to underwrite would be subject to the provisions on underwriting in Articles 11 and 13.

3. In paragraph 1, subparagraph (iii), Delegates did not intend this provision to prevent the Bank using private placement or other means of disposing of securities in which it had invested, if an adequate secondary market in those securities did not exist.

4. Delegates agreed that the authority specified in sub-paragraph (iv) of this Article to guarantee securities in which the Bank had invested should not be used in the case of securities which the Bank had acquired as part of its liquidity investments.

ARTICLE 24

Delegates agreed that the Bank would bear the cost of remuneration of not more than four people working full time on Bank matters, in respect of each Directorship.

ARTICLE 26

1. In paragraph 2 of this Article, Delegates hoped that as far as possible Directors would also have a wide and well balanced knowledge of Central and Eastern Europe, so as to contribute competently to the Bank's purpose and functions as set out in Articles 1 and 2 and to fulfil competently their obligations in paragraph 3 of Article 8.

2. Delegates recognised the importance for the original member countries from recipient countries listed in Annex A of maintaining at least four Directors for this group, so as to allow each such country either its own Director or its own Alternate in the event that the list of such countries is modified. Delegates agreed that in deciding to increase or decrease the size, or revise the composition of the Board of Directors, in order to take into account changes in the number of the members of the Bank, as provided in paragraph 3 of this Article, the Board of Governors should take account of this wish.

3. Delegates agreed that Directors and their Alternates should be resident at the headquarters of the Bank.

ARTICLE 28

In paragraph 3, Delegates noted that usual practice in other International Financial Institutions was not to permit a prospective borrower specially to be represented at the Board.

ARTICLE 29

1. Delegates intended that members whose payments, including encashment of promissory notes, fell short of the full amount due on the relevant dates to the Bank in respect of their paid-in shares should forfeit the corresponding percentage of their voting power unless and until the shortfall was made good.

2. The intention in paragraph 3 was to allow split voting by Directors representing more than one member, without making such voting obligatory.

3. Delegates intended that, in the case of differing views on whether or not issues involved "general policy", decisions would be made by the Board on the basis of advice from the Legal Counsel. In general, decisions on individual operations would not involve such issues, but "general policy issues" would include, *inter alia*, the budget; the annual programme of operations; borrowing policy, including borrowing limits; interest rate policy; exchange risk management policy; the drawing down of notes; underwriting policy and the organizational structure of the Bank.

ARTICLE 30

Delegates intended that men and women should be given equal opportunities in the recruitment process and in terms of service, training, promotion and career development generally.

ARTICLE 35

1. Delegates agreed that there was no need to have a provision about working languages in the Articles. The letter from the Conference Chairman to all Delegates (copy attached to this Report) sets out the understanding of Delegates about working languages.

2. Delegates were conscious that there might be little to report initially on the Bank's environmental impact and that the form of the first annual reports on this subject might be very different from later versions.

ARTICLE 36

Delegates were of the view that the principle behind paragraph 2 was that the distribution of cash should be strictly proportional to the cash payments made by each member, and the notes encashed, in respect of its paid-in shares.

ARTICLE 39

In paragraph 2, Delegates envisaged that all potential new members would join the Bank by subscribing to share capital at par value, with no account being taken of accumulated reserves. Delegates were thus concerned that those who later chose to leave the Bank for any reason should not profit unduly by so doing, or indeed have any profit incentive to do so, in the event of the book value of their shares having greatly increased since their original purchase. The wording of this paragraph therefore had the aim of ensuring that they should not get back more than they had paid in. The reference to "shown by the books of the Bank" could permit adjustments in Bank financial statements to reflect current and accumulated losses.

ARTICLE 46

Delegates noted that this Article was almost exactly the same as Section 3 of Article VII of the I.B.R.D.'s Articles of Agreement. They hoped that courts construing it would draw on the jurisprudence that had evolved in connection with the I.B.R.D.'s Articles.

ARTICLE 52

Delegates accepted paragraph 2 of Article 52 in the light of the locations then being considered for Bank operations.

ARTICLES 51 AND 55

These Articles were worded to reflect recent international thinking and practice, in accordance with the strong wishes of many Delegates.

ARTICLE 53

1. With respect to Article 53, paragraphs 1, 2 and 3, Delegates shared the view that members would accord the greatest deference to the Bank on whether a Bank activity was "official" or whether a purchase of goods and services was "necessary" for the "official" activities of the Bank; e.g. a duly authorized purchase of goods is to be presumed as "necessary" for the "official" activities of the Bank. Beyond this, Delegates shared the view that paragraph 2 was to be interpreted in the light of national practices applicable to international organizations with similar provisions.

2. It was accepted that nothing in Article 53 was to be interpreted as preventing any member from granting greater exemption from taxation than that provided for in this Article.

3. It was the common understanding of Delegates that "duties" referred to in paragraph 2 does not include customs duties, whilst "import duties" and "export duties", in paragraph 3, include customs duties.

4. In paragraph 6, Delegates understood that the "internal effective tax" was not a tax as that term is commonly used in tax treaties, national tax practice and so forth, and was not a tax which is imposed in the exercise of sovereign power. In addition they understood that the Bank's contracts of employment would contain provisions regarding the "internal effective tax".

5. With respect to paragraphs 6 and 7, Delegates shared the view that the Bank will regularly inform the members concerned, according to arrangements made with such members, of the amount of the salaries and emoluments paid to its Directors, Alternates, officers and employees in order to enable them to tax those salaries and emoluments (paragraph 7) or to tax properly the income from other sources than the exempt salaries and emoluments (paragraph 6).

6. Delegates took note of the importance placed by some members on their right to tax income derived by their residents who are officers or employees of the Bank. The provisions of paragraphs 6 and 7 of Article 53 do not preclude these members from lodging appropriate reservations in accordance with international law.

ARTICLES 60 AND 61

Delegates intended that these Articles should be read in conjunction with Article 3. Prospective members who sign the Agreement by the date specified in Article 60 and who deposit instruments of ratification, acceptance or approval by the date specified in paragraph 1 or paragraph 2 of Article 61, shall become parties to the Agreement in accordance with the Articles and shall, *inter alia*, be entitled to subscribe to the number of shares allocated to them in Annex A. The terms and conditions of membership of prospective members who sign the Agreement after the date specified in Article 60 and/or who deposit their instruments of ratification, acceptance or approval later than the date in paragraphs 1 or 2 of Article 61 will be determined by the Bank in accordance with paragraph 2 of Article 3. In respect of the initial shares to be subscribed to by such members, paragraph 2 of Article 3 should be read in conjunction with paragraph 2 of Article 5.

ARTICLE 62

Delegates intended, immediately after the adoption of the Agreement by Heads of Delegations, to start discussion on the possibility of transitional arrangements allowing the operations of the Bank to start as soon as possible after the date of entry into force of that Agreement.

Appendix VI

Letter from the Chairman of the Conference to All Delegations

During our discussions about the European Bank for Reconstruction and Development, we agreed to follow the normal practice of making no reference to the working languages in the Bank's Statutes. This letter is therefore to record the understanding we reached together, that the four languages of the authentic text of the Agreement, mentioned in the testimonium, would be the Bank's working languages, to be used by the Bank according to its day to day needs, and taking into consideration the interest of efficiency and economy.

Appendix VII

List of Signatories of the Agreement

Australia
Austria
Belgium
Bulgaria
Canada
Cyprus
Czechoslovakia
Denmark
Egypt
European Economic Community
European Investment Bank
Finland
France
German Democratic Republic
Germany, Federal Republic of
Greece
Hungary
Iceland
Ireland
Israel
Italy
Japan
Korea, Republic of
Liechtenstein
Luxembourg
Malta
Mexico
Morocco
Netherlands
New Zealand
Norway
Poland
Portugal
Romania
Spain
Sweden
Switzerland
Turkey
U.S.S.R.
United Kingdom
United States
Yugoslavia

Index